Praise for Representative Democracy:

Past, present, and future have no borders: "Many people", Nietzsche observed, "are obstinate about the path once it is taken, few people about the destination." Marques Mendes´ s book has the virtue of giving a meaning to the concept of democracy as a destination. Our liberal democracies, he states, have a "tiring nature". And he adds: "Democracy is not about governance. It´s a pact we make – an agreement to look out for everyone´s rights and interests." That´s why voting is not an insurance in itself. Many tyrants got to power by election. Jorge Luis Borges said once: No me gusta la democracia porque suele elegir tiranos. Democracy is the guarantee of freedom, or it signifies nothing. Returning to Tocqueville, after two centuries of authoritarianism that advocated the exchange of freedom for social protection, democracy is, prima facie, political liberalism.
Amadeu Lopes Sabino
Portuguese Writer
Former Director at the EU Council of Ministers.

Will representative democracy withstand threats like corruption, wealth inequality, populism, and the rise of AI, or will it succumb to them? The knowledge that the only true alternatives are dictatorship and chaos may no more be a powerful enough deterrent. Changes are needed. Marques-Mendes dares to dissect all those diseases and to point out ways, if not of curing them, at least of opening new paths for their discussion – in some cases in unexpected ways. His captivating style captures readers. The book is a roadmap to the eternal adventure of preserving democracy.

Manuel Regalado,
Former CFO of Navigator Company SA.

Other pillars for the good of humanity:

Pillar I: Enlightenment Virtues,

Pillar II: Constitutional Liberalism,

Pillar IV: Science and Reason,

Pillar V: Productive Work,

Pillar VI: Market Capitalism.

Also published by SADIF Investment Analytics.

Six Pillars for the Good of Humanity

Pillar III:

Representative Democracy

Antonio J. Marques-Mendes

ANTONIO J. MARQUES-MENDES

Published by: SADIF Investment Analytics, Ilhavo, Portugal

Cover page by Fabio Soares

DEDICATION

To the many victims of tyranny.

ACKNOWLEDGMENTS

Without beating around the bush, let's be honest - this book wouldn't have come to fruition if not for a glorious cocktail of retirement leisure and the wondrous aid of ChatGPT. I owe a debt of gratitude to Lucy Kellaway, who graciously tolerated my appropriation of her stylistic wizardry. Don't get your knickers in a twist though - her tolerance doesn't equate to an endorsement of my views.

Let's not forget my steadfast supporters - family, friends, and colleagues, who've patiently endured my absenteeism while pumping me up with their encouraging words. In keeping with time-honored tradition, the blame game ends with me. If there are errors, misconceptions, or omissions lurking in these pages, they are entirely on my head. A gentleman never shies away from taking responsibility, after all.

viii

CONTENTS

ANTONIO J. MARQUES-MENDES

INTRODUCTION

Back in the chilly grasp of February 2010, I rolled up my sleeves and decided to kick off my now dormant blogging saga on the 'Six Pillars for the Good of Humanity' (have a peek at http://marques-mendes.blogspot.com/). At that point, the glamorous choice for one of these pillars was as obvious as a neon sign - representative democracy. The decision had its roots both in the fertile soil of theory and the rocky terrain of personal experience.

Personally, I've weathered life's storms in Portugal, under the stern gaze of Salazar's authoritarian rule during my salad days, and later under a democracy, albeit of the socialist variety, during my adult years. Both systems, though neither a poster child for dictatorship nor an epitome of democracy, offered a rich educational journey through the potholes and detours of democracy's imperfect avatars.

Still, the theoretical basis was the ace up my sleeve, tipping the scales towards studying the fascinating paradox of mankind's predatory streak squaring off against the global sway of representative democracy. History's pages are smeared with the fingerprints of dictatorships and authoritarian regimes, a stark reflection of humanity's predatory instincts. Yet, we have traded in our cudgels for keyboards, and despite our predatory legacy, find ourselves in an era that's considerably more civilized. This begs the question - can democracy be our silver bullet to tame our inner predator?

Predation, the natural order of the food chain, is a common spectacle in the biosphere. And we humans are no strangers to it. As omnivores, we've played the predator, armed with weapons and tools, in our relentless pursuit for sustenance, fishing, hunting, and trapping our way to survival. Furthermore, we often feed our desires on the fruits of other humans' labour. To retain our throne at the apex of the predatory hierarchy, it's vital we possess the power to fend off competition.

Hence, the power gambit and its unique playbook form the stalwart skeleton of a robust ecosystem. Picture this: you could amass power through a hodgepodge of means - a lucrative inheritance, a heroic conquest, a landslide election victory, or if you're on a lucky streak, the lottery. Plus, the wielding of power is an art form - it can range from the unassailable absolute to the inclusive participative, from the restrained limited to the ephemeral temporary. In a nutshell, the cornucopia of potential political setups rivals the colour spectrum in its diversity.

In the lively realm of my blog, I've busily scribbled on democracy, interspersed with ruminations on other political conundrums and scientific musings. However, considering the labyrinthine nature of some topics, a lightbulb moment occurred - perhaps readers would find a book, neatly laying out the democracy discourse in a logical thread, useful.

Behold, the literary offspring of my tenacious pursuit, sprouting forth from the very essence of contemplation. This opus, painstakingly crafted amidst fits and starts, encountered numerous halts along its arduous path. Indeed, its final form would have remained elusive had it not been for the advent of ChatGPT, a revolutionary tool. With its aid, the barren gaps within were swiftly filled within a mere fortnight, ushering in a transformative metamorphosis of the entire tome, adopting the witty prose of Lucy Kellaway, a renowned British journalist, author, and former columnist for the Financial Times. Thus, my once monotonously scholarly style was seamlessly replaced by a tapestry of utter delight.

Initially, trepidation gripped my being, for I feared accusations of intellectual larceny. However, providence smiled upon me as the esteemed Lucy Kellaway herself responded to my tweet, sanctioning this audacious endeavor with the words, " "Great idea. Might do it myself."

So, here is a text where passages are succinct, favouring plain English over jargon-laden language. The crispness might raise an eyebrow or two given the complexity of the topics. Peppered throughout are original ideas that, by rights, ought to have seen the light of day in peer-reviewed scholarly journals.

The book is neatly parcelled into three segments - foundations, the art of collective decision making, and the hurdles lining the path of representative democracy.

The opening act, 'Foundations of representative democracy' (chapters 1-5), gets the ball rolling with an exploration of democracy, followed by a whistle-stop tour of its six pivotal institutions. It then delves into the major strains of democracy and rounds off with a probing analysis of the seedbed of anti-democratic ideologies.

Next, the curtain lifts on 'collective decision-making' (chapters 6-9), painting it as more than just an economic mechanism. It emerges as a pivotal gear in the machinery of freedom, democracy, and equality - the very ideals that are often weaponized to vilify capitalism.

The grand finale, 'challenges to representative democracy' (chapters 10-12), puts the spotlight on the boogeymen lurking within the belly of popular democracy.

I've tailored this book to appeal to a broad swath of readers, but every now and then, my professional leanings elbow their way in, particularly my penchant for financial matters. To those readers for whom financial jargon is about as thrilling as watching paint dry, feel free to hit fast-forward on those sections.

By and large, the insights scattered throughout the pages are my own musings that I've tossed into the mix. My aim? To stir up a stimulating mental gymnastics routine for you, dear reader.

1 Political Systems and Democracy

Welcome to a romp through the murky world of political systems and democracy. This chapter is a helter-skelter tour through the madhouse of politics, whizzing from the grunts and gesturing of prehistoric tribal meetings to the sleek, complex, and often just as incomprehensible, machinations of our modern global village. Why? To reveal what on earth the state and government have to do with all of this.

The escapade kicks off with a nose dive into the past, sifting through the dirt and disorder of hunter-gatherer societies, serfdom, monarchy, communism, and capitalism. We're aiming to unearth the guts of these systems - the who's who of power, the ideologies that kept the lights on, and the societal scaffolding. This dusty delve should give us a nice torch to shine on today's world and the role of our beloved state and government.

Next, we'll scrutinize the state's identity crisis. The state is a classic overthinker. Flex too much muscle, and it suffocates the life out of individual freedom and start-ups. Play too shy, and the weakest risk getting trampled. This chapter dissects this tricky tightrope walk between helicopter-parent state and laissez-faire laissez-aller.

After this, brace yourself for the roller-coaster saga of democracy, from its baby steps in ancient Athens to its teenage angst and global spread. We'll pore over the bumps, loop-de-loops, and straight runs, along with its many mood swings. From the no-nonsense direct democracy of Swiss villages to the delegate dance of larger nations, we'll investigate how democracy's moulded itself to fit the times.

As we burrow into democracy, it becomes painfully clear we're in need of a better chat. With the hot mess of climate change and wealth gaps, do we need a spring clean of the system for better informed, inclusive decision-making? Or are we facing a teenage rebellion against democratic parents?

Lastly, we'll face what many call the final boss of democracy: fair re-elections. But we're not stopping at the voting booth; we'll dig into other must-haves like freedom of speech, rule of law, and keeping Big Brother in check.

So, fasten your seatbelts for this intellectual roller coaster. As we hurtle through the history, kerfuffles, and brainwaves of political systems and democracy, we're gunning to boost your understanding and fire up some good old chinwags on where we're heading in this whirligig world.

A whirlwind tour of political systems

Before we lay the foundation for discussing democracy - irrespective of the definition you're partial to - we need to turn back the pages of history and examine the annals of political systems. By political systems, I mean the matrix of institutions (the political machinery) and forms of government (the control mechanisms). Four elemental questions form the bedrock of this investigation: 1) who's on the receiving end of the rule; 2) who's holding the reins; 3) what's in their governance portfolio; and 4) what's their governance style?

Those being governed are usually communities woven from clans or sprawling family trees, tribes, or nations, all nestled within specific territories.

The puppet masters, the ones orchestrating policies - be they lawmakers, administrators, or arbitrators - are those wielding the power baton over the governed.

The sphere of governance is a veritable smorgasbord, spanning legal, economic, social, and cultural fields. And the rules? They can be etched in stone or understood implicitly.

And then, there's the matter of power - its acquisition and application can range from mild to wild and from dictatorial to collaborative.

The tapestry of human history is embroidered with a plethora of ways these four elements intermingle, often under the influence of diverse factors like religion, affluence, and ideologies, shaping political structures. It's also worth noting that certain types of governance are better suited to particular political contexts. Take, for instance, market capitalism - it struts its stuff best under a democratic umbrella.

In the fleeting historical snapshot that follows, we'll rely on the economic systems classification outlined in our previous work, 'The Beauty of Capitalism' (Marques Mendes, 2016). We'll trot through the eras of hunter-gatherers, predatory societies, slave economies, serfdom, central planning, and capitalism. And for the flavours of government, we'll pick from the menu of the MaxRange rating (Max Rånge and Mikael Sandberg, 2014), featuring absolutism, anarchy, despotism, colonial rule, totalitarianism, military rule, authoritarianism, democracy, and a mixed bag of others.

Let's kick off with the dawn of civilization - hunter-gatherer communities made up of clans and compact tribes. It's widely held that power, in such settings, was typically rooted in bloodlines, seeped into all aspects of daily life - from cradle to grave - and was brandished with an iron fist.

Toss out the idea that anarchy is anything more than a political daydream about a world sans government. It's like hoping for an office without a boss. The few times we've dipped our toes into it, things went a bit wild west and quickly spiralled into some form of dictatorship, like the office prankster suddenly claiming the corner office.

The early dog-eat-dog societies eventually smartened up and, in a rather dark twist, opted for economies built on the backs of slaves and serfs. When farming took off, society neatly divided itself into the fat cats sitting on their land and the worker bees toiling away on it. The overlords skimmed the cream off the top and the proletariat found themselves working for their masters' benefit - a nasty bit of business justified by despotism or absolutism, where one entity played God.

Next, the colonial rule swept in, a classic power play dictated by the colonisers' pocketbook and politics. Often, a side of military rule was served up, ensuring a rich tapestry of inequality and resource exploitation. Different dressings, same salad - the little guys were suppressed for the advantage of a privileged few.

Come the 20th century, and we saw central planning with socialism and communism strutting onto the scene, all gung-ho about controlling the production strings. But totalitarian rule turned out to be a party pooper. Despite its siren song of perfect equality, it often ushered in dictatorships that squashed freedom and innovation like an unwelcome bug.

And then, capitalism sauntered in, arm in arm with democracy. Capitalism sets the economy to the beat of supply and demand, and democracy hands out political freedom like sweets. However, even capitalism, the poster child for egalitarianism, has a dark side. The rich-poor divide looms large, leaving an underclass grappling to be heard in the democratic chorus.

Across the smorgasbord of governmental systems, power is the unrelenting constant, but its dish varies from tyranny to democracy. Like hunting for the perfect espresso blend, the ideal form is elusive. Perhaps it's a mix of these systems that acknowledges the complexity of the human brew. So, the quest for a balanced power distribution, respecting personal freedom while catering to collective wellbeing, remains on the menu.

State and government: Unmasking their roles

Debates on the role of the state can often resemble a rather messy food fight - data flung around haphazardly and political rhetoric in full swing.

Take, for instance, the Portuguese government in 2013. They dressed up a four billion Euros slash in public expenditure, under the aegis of an agreement with the IMF, as a grand "refoundation of the state". But it smacked more of a game of musical chairs, a case of "scoot over so I can perch there". Bafflingly, the government, in the same breath, dug into borrowed funds to establish a new development bank. In a country where the state already has a lion's share of over 50% of the banking sector, birthing yet another state-run development bank - a model that's already taken a nosedive both in Portugal and globally - smacks of either a skilful sleight of hand or downright recklessness.

In a nutshell, the Portuguese government's call to arms for a debate on the role of government rings hollow and would usually not merit a second glance. However, a genuine pow-wow on the state's role is too critical to be sidelined and ought to be a staple of political banter.

As Martin Wolf penned in his piece on the topic in 2010, it is "the most important issue of political economy" - a theme that's been tossed around since the days of Plato and his philosopher buddies. Wolf's spotlight on the scope and limitations of the state's protective role is rather riveting and worth a read.

To elevate such a discourse beyond mere intellectual shadow boxing, one needs a firm grasp of the state's current role - in terms of function, cost, and contribution to the national coffers.

Public expenditure, for instance, is usually sliced and diced into ten categories, as seen in the accompanying table for Portugal.

		Country	Portugal				
		Sector	GS13: General government				
		Measure	Current prices				
		Transaction	TLYCG: Total government				
		Unit	Euro, Millions				
		Year	1996	2006	2011	2016	2021
B1_GE: Gross domestic product (expenditure approach)			94,351.6	166,260.5	176,096.2	186,489.8	214,741.0
T: Total function			43.1%	45.2%	50.0%	44.8%	47.7%
010: General public services			8.6%	6.7%	8.9%	8.2%	6.8%
010: General public services	0107: Public debt transactions		4.9%	2.9%	4.5%	4.3%	2.5%
020: Defence			1.7%	1.3%	1.2%	0.9%	0.8%
030: Public order and safety			1.6%	1.9%	2.0%	1.8%	1.8%
040: Economic affairs			5.1%	4.4%	4.5%	3.2%	5.5%
040: Economic affairs	0405: Transport		2.7%	2.4%	2.4%	1.9%	2.3%
050: Environment protection			0.6%	0.7%	0.7%	0.6%	0.8%
060: Housing and community amenities			0.8%	0.7%	0.4%	0.4%	0.6%
070: Health			5.7%	7.1%	7.0%	6.1%	7.6%
070: Health	0703: Hospital services		2.8%	3.7%	4.0%	3.4%	4.2%
080: Recreation, culture and religion			1.1%	1.1%	1.2%	0.8%	1.0%
090: Education			5.8%	6.4%	6.1%	4.8%	4.6%
100: Social protection			12.2%	15.1%	18.0%	18.1%	18.3%
100: Social protection	1002: Old age		5.7%	8.8%	11.5%	12.2%	11.9%
	1005: Unemployment		0.7%	1.1%	1.2%	0.8%	0.8%

Data extracted on 14 Jul 2023 15:46 UTC (GMT) from OECD.Stat

But such a breakdown doesn't quite capture the essence of the state's functions. A more enlightening way to categorize the state's role would be into five main tasks: sovereignty, regulation, insurance, production, and distribution.

Each activity, for better or worse, leaves an imprint on the different public expenditure categories outlined in the table, but their budgetary footprint doesn't always paint the full picture. Regulation, for example, might barely dent the budget but can exact a hefty economic toll. And there can be budgeting anomalies - in Portugal, for instance, not all the fees coughed up to regulators make it onto the budget. Similarly, the state's role in wealth redistribution can be executed either through income or expenditure.

But this typical breakdown is hardly the best route to fathom the state's functions. We should rather slice them into five key duties: sovereignty, regulation, insurance, production, and distribution. These activities, for all their virtues and vices, ripple through the various public expenditure categories we find in the table above.

We could also mull over if the insurance, production, and distribution activities should be entrusted to the state or farmed out to private entities. For instance, why do we contract out construction services in public works and not educational services? In other words, the debate on whether the state should be a producer versus a provider should be kept separate from the discourse on the state's functions.

Above all, we need to tease apart the insurance and redistribution roles of the state. Whether we're talking health, unemployment, or weather insurance, we must draw a clear line between a compulsory insurance component (subsidized or not by the state) and a discretionary component funded by taxes to handle curveballs (epidemics, natural disasters, etc.).

When it comes to life insurance and pensions, beyond subsidization, the critical conversation should revolve around the floor and ceiling levels. Should the State be playing Santa to millionaires, offering them pension insurance? Given the hefty slice of public spending that pensions gobble up, this might just be the juiciest debate when it comes to the state's role.

To nutshell it, a meaty, well-seasoned debate on the boundaries of the state's role necessitates a dissection of public expenditure and its financing by each of the five state activities. Setting up an accounting system that enables such an analysis should be top of the to-do list for any government keen on a serious discourse on the state's functions.

Only once we've agreed upon the constraints

in each state activity should we dive into the issues related to the relative efficacy of direct versus delegated administration. Additionally, we need to address how to tackle the free-riding, theft, and nepotism that are the customary villains in any political system.

Too much or too little state?

In the spectator sport of public sentiment, Keynes often gets labelled the champion of state intervention, while Hayek gets pegged as the embodiment of laissez-faire economics. It's as though we're looking at two caricatures, not the complex realities of these esteemed economists.

For Keynes, whose manifesto found its home in his 'General Theory', the role of the government was akin to that of an orchestra conductor, harmonising the propensity to consume with the inducement to invest, in order to ward off the spectre of deficient demand. He envisaged a state that sets the production volume dial (with full employment as the dream destination), leaving the 'what', 'how' and 'for whom' to the discretion of individuals.

Hayek, on the other hand, eyed terms like full employment, planning, social security, and freedom from want with the scepticism one reserves for mirages. In his view, these phrases often served as trojan horses, harbinger of calamity. Take, for example, Germany's brag-worthy 'full employment' from 1935 to 1939, bought at the unthinkable price of expropriating, deporting, or killing 600,000 Jews. Hayek contended that monetary policy couldn't be the magic pill for unemployment, without unleashing an inflation beast. And when others saw the rising monopolisation of the early twentieth century as an inevitable offshoot of capitalism, born from economies of scale or technological necessities, Hayek saw the hidden hand of collusive agreements between firms, egged on by public policies.

Given the turbulent waters of the times they navigated, it's no wonder that Keynes fretted over recurrent, mammoth unemployment sinking the ship of capitalism, while Hayek sounded the alarm on the iceberg of a totalitarian state looming ahead, courtesy of increasing government control. But, with the clarity that comes with hindsight and eight decades of distance, we can wonder if these anxieties were overblown.

After all, the sun has set on many a totalitarian regime, either through military defeat (think German Nazis, Italian Fascists), internal implosion driven by inefficiency (Communism in Soviet

Union and Eastern Europe) or a morphing into an authoritarian mercantilist capitalism, effectively postponing their swan song (Chinese communists, I'm looking at you).

Similarly, the storm clouds of recessions and the torrential rains of massive unemployment have been weathered, without the feared societal tempest, partly due to the umbrella of unemployment insurance.

However, let's not sweep under the rug the colossal wreckage left behind by such collectivist experiments. The nightmarish toll of over 60 million lives claimed by Hitler's initiated World War II, the 15 million victims swallowed up in Stalin's reign of terror in the 1930s, and Mao's over 20 million victims during the grisly periods of the so-called Great Leap Forward and the Cultural Revolution in the 1950s and 1960s.

And let's not forget the squandering of human potential resulting from rampant involuntary unemployment in many nations under the yoke of collectivist regimes (mainly socialist) in recent history. In 2009, for instance, Zimbabwe bore the dubious distinction of 95% unemployment, trailed by Turkmenistan (60%), South Africa (24%), Spain (19%), and Tunisia (16%).

Surveying the wreckage of our rather bleak

historical landscape, one can't help but wonder: if the principles championed by Keynes and Hayek had been treated like stars to navigate by, rather than mere twinkles in the vast economic cosmos, could we have sidestepped some of the suffering and waste? Could the scorching impacts of poor policies have been turned into mere singes? The answer, unsurprisingly, is a resounding 'yes'. If not outright dodging, at least a savvy sidestep could have been managed, especially if the acolytes of Keynes and Hayek had followed suit in their reverence for capitalism.

Yet, many of these supposed disciples shrugged off this common ground, turning a blind eye to both the crumbling edifice of past prophecies predicting the demise of capitalism, as well as its tenacious refusal to keel over. All these theories, from Karl Marx's Surplus-Value Theory, foretelling an inevitable capital pile-up, to Schumpeter's forecast of capitalism birthing a hostile corporatist culture, to Milton Friedman's proclamation of capitalism's innate death-wish, right through to Solzhenitsyn's critique of capitalism's commodification of Western culture, have been left red-faced.

Even more eye-opening is the fiasco of attempts to cobble together a supposedly "third way", a Goldilocks solution, intending to cherry-pick the best of socialism and capitalism. From

Tony Blair's New Labor experiment in Britain, to the Czech and Hungarian forays into democratic socialism in 1968 and 1956, to the Fascist 'third way' of the 1930s, these attempts ended up spectacularly backfiring. They managed to seize the worst of both systems, spawning more corruption, tyranny, inequality, and collectivism.

For both Keynes and Hayek, there was no secret shortcut, no hidden pathway. Capitalism was the road well-trodden, and the question was merely about how much of a co-driver role the government should play. Whether evaluating the provision of goods and services not catered to by the private sector, or scrutinising regulations aimed at ensuring a fair game, Keynes, the seasoned political player, was more at ease with the government in the passenger seat. Hayek, the purist scholar, preferred a leaner co-driver.

Some flavours of state capitalism, the Scandinavian recipe, for instance, have demonstrated that Hayek's nightmarish vision of authoritarianism spurred on by increased state involvement doesn't take form until the public spending dial is cranked up to around 50% of GDP. Similarly, the government's beefed-up role does offer a certain soothing balm to the erratic swings of the business cycle, as Keynes advocated, but once that 50% threshold is crossed, it's like hitting an economic speed bump, leading to productivity and economic decline.

So, in essence, Keynes and Hayek were both on the money within a certain ballpark of state intervention. But defining the boundaries of this ballpark without considering the specifics of the situation is as misguided as a game of blindfolded darts.

From ancient Athens to the global village

Picture Athens, 4th century BC, when the seeds of democracy were first sown. The notion was downright scandalous! The idea that commoners, not just kings or the well-heeled, should have a say in the affairs of state, seemed like letting the lunatics run the asylum.

The Athenian democracy was not a tea party. It was raw and participatory, with all free-born males joining the decision-making chorus. Not to put too fine a point on it, but women, slaves, and foreign settlers didn't get a look in, leaving this early democracy looking more than a little undemocratic by today's standards.

Spreading this "mad" idea around took its sweet time. Conventional wisdom then dictated that the hoi polloi simply didn't have the smarts to govern. Plus, for ages, the top brass and blue bloods clung to power like limpets to a rock.

Come the 20th century, the global mood music began to change. The churn of the industrial revolution, the rising tide of education and a middle class hungry for a slice of the political pie were a potent mix. The horrors of two world wars pulled the rug out from under autocratic regimes, nudging people towards a more equitable rule of the roost. And let's not forget the heady days of decolonization, sparking a rash of new-born nations giddy on democratic principles.

Fast forward to the 21st century, democracy is the new black. Be it the representative flavor, where we elect others to do our bidding, it's the governance style du jour. But let's not get too starry-eyed. Democracy worldwide is more a patchwork quilt than a perfectly smooth fabric. Corruption, muzzled voices, and trampled opposition parties leave noticeable wrinkles in many nations.

Yet, despite the gnarly bits, democracy is showing some serious staying power. People around the world, championing for their rights and freedoms, have kept the democratic spirit alive and kicking. In our digital age, the scope for citizen engagement has exploded, potentially making democracy even more robust.

So, here's the thing. Democracy may have been a late bloomer, taking its own sweet time to come into its own. Its core values of freedom, equality, and representation remain as appealing as a hot cup of tea on a cold day. Sure, we have hurdles, but they remind us that democracy isn't a destination but a journey – one that requires our constant attention and an insatiable appetite for equality. And isn't that a journey worth taking?

Democracy's roller-coaster ride

Picture this: democracy, the grand dame of the political system, pulling off a stunning comeback, with Britain taking the lead, before sashaying across Europe and the United States. The cataclysmic events of World War II, the great decolonization shuffle, and the spectacular belly flop of communism, all served as wind beneath democracy's wings. But, and it's a big but, our darling democracy has run into a rough patch lately, getting a punch in the gut from the trio of populism, proto-fascism, and self-serving politicos.

Back in the 17th century, Britain decided to kick the tires of democracy with the Glorious

Revolution. The throne had to share the limelight with Parliament, and the twin forces of representation and constitutionalism moved in. Not to be outdone, Europe started cozying up to these ideals, nudged along by Enlightenment thinkers hollering for equality, liberty, and fraternity.

Meanwhile, over in the U.S., they embraced democracy like a long-lost friend. The American Revolution in 1776 ushered in a republic, waving the flag for democratic principles. The U.S. Constitution became the poster child for checks and balances, individual rights, and the rule of law, now must-haves in any democratic setup.

After the bloodbath of World War II, democracy started looking pretty good. Autocratic ideologies took a nosedive, and both the U.S. and Britain became cheerleaders for democracy, breathing life back into battered Europe through the Marshall Plan.

As colonies started breaking free post-war, democracy rode the wave. Fresh-faced nations in Africa, Asia, and the Caribbean, either inspired by their former overlords or hankering for self-rule, started sporting democratic stripes.

The late 20th century saw communism hit the skids, giving democracy another shot in the arm.

As the Berlin Wall crumbled and the Soviet Union unraveled, Eastern Europe bid adieu to one-party rule, opening the doors to democracy.

But here's the kicker: our darling democracy is getting a bit of a drubbing these days. Populism, fed by economic woes and social discord, is thumbing its nose at democratic norms. Populist leaders, armed with divisive rhetoric, are busily undermining the principles of pluralism.

At the same time, proto fascism is muscling in. This ugly duckling, with its dictatorial swagger and penchant for suppressing opposition, threatens to leave democracy in tatters. It's become a darling of leaders who tighten their grip by stoking fear and division, trampling over democratic values of equality and respect for individual rights.

And let's not forget the threat from within. Professional politicians, putting self and party before public, are helping erode trust in democratic processes.

So, here's the rub: democracy, from its British awakening, has weathered many storms. It's now up against some formidable foes. To keep the democratic spirit alive, we've got to face down populism and proto-fascism and call out politicians who play fast and loose with the public interest. Lessons from the past can inform the present, steering democracy's course. Despite current challenges, democracy's staying power speaks volumes about its enduring appeal. However, safeguarding it demands our unflagging vigilance, active participation, and unwavering commitment to democratic principles.

Better deliberations: "Reform or rebellion?"

Drawing conclusions from my discourse, it seems glaringly obvious that the sun is setting on Portugal's left-leaning state capitalism. Not only because it's threatening to outstay its welcome, matching the shelf life of the authoritarian Estado Novo, but also because the regime's future looks as precarious as a house of cards under the scrutinising gaze of foreign creditors, who wield their power through a series of 'adjustment' programs, brokered with the Troika.

What follows could be a regime change, either to a system of market capitalism, managed economics, or a U-turn to right-wing (think corporate, or oligarchic à la Putin) or left-wing state capitalism (with a third-worldist tinge, as we've seen with Chavez or the Angolan model).

The winds of change will partly be guided by whether the champions of these various regimes choose the path of the reformist (democracy's sweetheart) or take a sharp turn down Revolution Avenue (military coup's stomping ground). Therefore, it's crucial to weigh up the potential of both routes. We're not looking to resuscitate the debate between Rosa Luxemburg and Bernstein on how to build socialism from the 19th-century archives. The task here is a simple, no-frills evaluation of the pros and cons of each regime change avenue.

Revolution comes with a certain allure. It dangles the promise of utopia, to be delivered with next day shipping. But here's the rub - while we may know how it kicks off, how it concludes is anyone's guess. History's back catalogue is replete with revolutions that promised the earth and delivered a punch in the gut.

On the other side of the spectrum, the reformist path often seems like a Herculean task, making Sisyphus's efforts look like a leisurely walk in the park. But it does bring to the table a certain potential for steady progression. The real feather in reform's cap is that it has a track record of getting to the finish line, especially if it's backed by strong, capable leadership.

From Whispers to Roars? In the Portuguese

politisphere, rumblings from the left (cue Otelo's rallying cry for a fresh 25th of April) and right are starting to make themselves heard, echoing a call for a modern-day Sidonism - a brand of nationalism that defies the Troika's reign and advocates for a return to protectionism. While the current regime is doing its best to juggle the corporate demands of the military, it's not entirely far-fetched that some might fancy playing their hand at a coup d'état, all in the name of 'temporarily' suspending democracy, amending the constitution, and upturning the political order.

From my perspective, the revolutionary route, apart from carrying the standard revolutionary risk bundle (civil war, anyone?), would almost inevitably perpetuate the reign of state capitalism. In other words, the only shift we'd see would be on the political stage. Hence, I'm rather sceptical that this approach could untangle the knots in Portuguese society.

Consequently, I champion the idea of marching towards political-economic change through reform. However, with the current state of Portuguese political parties, how does one navigate this path? I posit two possibilities. The first, usher in a party leader with an impressive absolute majority, who embodies the spirit of the enlightened despot. The second, elect a President by a landslide majority, who's firmly committed to bringing political parties to heel in the name of regime change.

Opting for the enlightened despot aligns neatly with Portugal's long-standing messianic tradition. After all, our illustrious reformers, like D. Afonso III, Marquês de Pombal, or Salazar, were all shining examples of this archetype. The fly in the ointment of this solution lies in the challenges of electing such leaders within a democratic regime, their slippery slope towards authoritarianism, and the question of whether their reforms will stand the test of time once they've exited the stage. While the first issue can be sidestepped by leaders who cleverly mask their reformist intentions until they've clinched power, ensuring the longevity of their reforms requires a genuine national commitment to their ideals. This is tricky ground because while despots have a knack for gathering a fanbase, they often fall short in leaving behind true disciples.

"So, it appears the surest, albeit the most treacherous, path to regime change lies in electing a President with limited powers. Sounds like a Herculean task, right? Not exactly impossible, if we consider the potential of a widespread mobilisation of intellectuals and society at large, rallying behind the principles of representative democracy, and the other keystones touted as the guarantors of human bliss.

Echoing the age-old adage – Rome wasn't built in a day – I'd argue the reformist transformation I champion won't magically materialise with a single presidential election. But isn't it the small steps that lead to grand renovations? So, let's consider this little essay as one such stride towards a national metamorphosis. Let's take this step together."

Test of democracy: Fair re-elections

If democracy were a party, freedom of choice, even the freedom to vote for the seemingly absurd, would be the star invitee. All the misfits, the tricksters, the power-hungry narcissists, they all get an invite too. That's the beauty and, perhaps, the madness of democracy. The real test, however, lies in whether they turn this party into a private soiree. Essentially, democracy has a bit of a balancing act to do: elections must be fair, the rule of law must stand tall, liberalism should be the flavour of the day, and self-regulation must be more than just a buzzword. Now, if we throw in a bit of controlled state interference in the economy, we might just have a recipe for a thriving democracy. Let's rummage through some global examples, shall we?

First up is India. The phrase 'world's largest

democracy' gets bandied about quite often with India, and there's a reason for that. Amidst the colourful chaos of diverse cultures and a plethora of political parties, India has consistently pulled off the high-wire act of free and fair elections. The process is meticulously supervised by an independent Election Commission that ensures the powerful can't simply plunder state resources for electoral gains. That said, the show's not without its stumbles. Money power, muscle power, political corruption, and an increasing state role in the economy all pose significant hurdles to the fairness of re-elections. Yet, thanks to robust democratic institutions and an assertive judiciary, the democracy extravaganza goes on.

Now, let's fly to Russia for a bit of a contrast. On paper, Russia is a democracy, but the ground reality is a stark departure. The fairness of the electoral process often finds itself in the critics' crosshairs. The script seems to be written by the incumbents, with opposition voices suppressed, media narratives controlled, and the electoral process 'managed'. Coupled with a monolithic state-controlled economy, the Russian narrative veers far from our democratic ideal.

Brazil, on the other hand, presents an interesting medley. It's a place that has danced to the tune of military rule and political instability but has somehow found its rhythm as a lively democracy. Elections are generally conducted with a fair hand, but the spectres of political corruption and the sway of powerful interest groups persist. Yet, with an independent judiciary and a free press setting the beat, Brazil's democracy hasn't missed a step, even managing to show two presidents the door.

These narratives from around the globe underline that the bedrock of fair re-elections is formed by strong democratic institutions, an unfaltering rule of law, liberalism, and self-regulation. But these elements alone don't cut the mustard. It takes an engaged and alert citizenry to keep the powers that be on their toes. And the state's dance card in the economy must be kept carefully limited to avoid power concentration and ensure a stage for competition, innovation, and economic freedom.

To wrap it up, the bellwether of democracy doesn't just lie in electing leaders, but in our capacity to give them a gracious exit through free and fair re-elections. The health of a democracy is measured through this prism of fair re-elections. Yes, every democracy is prone to an assortment of loons, charlatans, and power-seekers, but what truly matters is the strength of our democratic bouncers to keep them in check. Maintaining the fairness of re-elections isn't a one-off job; it's a relentless endeavour, one that calls for continuous vigilance, active participation, and a dogged commitment to democratic principles. As such, fair re-elections are more than just a marker of a functioning democracy; they're a reminder of the persistent work needed to uphold democratic ideals in power.

2 The Fundamental Institutions of Democracy

Welcome, dear reader, to an enlightening dive into democracy's nuts and bolts, the lifeblood of all democratic societies. Democracy, with its motley collection of principles - free and fair elections, freedom in all its dazzling forms, the rule of law, and universal suffrage - stands tall and distinct in the political landscape. This chapter offers a guided tour, stripped of jargon, loaded with insights.

Kicking things off, we pull back the curtains on elections, the dazzling showpiece of democracy. We'll get our hands dirty, digging into the elements that make an election both fair and free, illuminating the intricate mechanisms that give citizens their star turn on the stage of governance.

From the razzle-dazzle of elections, we saunter onto the vast terrain of freedom. Not just the freedom to pick out your own socks in the morning, but the heady freedoms of speech, press, and assembly. These freedoms are the hardy perennials in the garden of democracy, cultivating a vibrant and healthy society.

Having breathed in the fresh air of freedom, we march to the drumbeat of the rule of law. This unsung hero keeps democracy on an even keel, holding everyone, from Joe Bloggs to top-ranking officials, to the same legal standard, batting away the spectre of corruption and power abuse.

In keeping with our law-and-order theme, we'll delve into the separation of powers. This ingenious blueprint prevents a monopoly of power, distributing it like a well-shuffled deck of cards among the executive, legislative, and judicial branches. It's our bulwark against tyranny and the midwife of checks and balances.

Next, we tip our hats to the universal vote, a game-changer that endows every adult citizen, regardless of bank balance or birth, with the right to vote, steering the ship of state.

We'll then tackle the thorny question of the military's role in democracy, a topic that tends to get the chins wagging. It's a complex dance, balancing potential power grabs with national security.

Shifting gears, we'll contemplate the fine balancing act between majority rule and minority rights. Democracy dances to the majority's tune, but it must also shield minorities from any majoritarian overreach.

We'll also chew over democracy and impeachment, the hammer in the toolkit of accountability, putting it under the microscope for a closer look.

And lastly, we'll spotlight politicians' accountability, an aspect of democratic governance that often slips through the cracks.

With these topics, we embark on a voyage of discovery, stripping democracy down to its fundamentals and marvelling at its complexities. So, prepare for an intellectual banquet, full of food for thought on the delicate machinery of the democratic system.

Fair and free elections

Government of the people, by the people, for the people. This form of government is achieved through majority rule by people's representatives, subject to the constitutional separation of powers and the rights of the minorities. Representatives are elected periodically on the basis of one person one vote.

We are often fed the romantic notion that representative democracy is the dazzling gem of modern governance. It paints a pretty picture where our elected officials are the dutiful mirrors of public will. For this to hold any water, there's a rather hefty proviso: elections need to be as clean as a new pin.

Now, the ingredients for such pristine elections involve a smorgasbord of ideal conditions: universal vote without a hint of coercion, election-related laws as solid as a rock, election boards with the impartiality of Lady Justice herself, and voter registers that are as accurate as an atomic clock.

To add to the mix, campaigns should be more serene than a meditation retreat - no violence, no intimidation, no bribery, and definitely no dipping into the government's sweet jar. As for the actual voting, it needs to be so secret it'd make a Masonic meeting look like an open book. The media, well, they should be as free as a bird to make candidates' laundry, both dirty and clean, a public spectacle.

And, not to forget, vote counting must be an open and honest affair. If not, we might as well put our faith in a three-card Monte dealer than the electoral process.

Sadly, elections around the world seem to have taken these criteria as a mere suggestion rather than gospel. Take the 2020 Belarusian presidential election, for example. The voting process there seemed less transparent than a brick wall, and voter fraud allegations spread faster than juicy office gossip. The subsequent public outcry would make a rock concert seem like a library. Then we have Zimbabwe and Uganda, both with a track record of elections resembling a poorly written thriller - full of violence, intimidation, and plot twists in the form of vote-rigging.

In a nutshell, if we ever want to see the blooming flower of representative democracy, our elections need to be free and fair. That includes everything from unswerving election laws, non-violent campaigns, secret voting, to open media access and transparent vote counting. Otherwise, we're just putting lipstick on a pig, calling it democracy. Thus, it's high time for all the movers and shakers, both locally and globally, to pull their socks up and set the gold standard for free and fair elections.

Freedom

Freedom, that heady mix of rights and privileges, is the yeast that makes the bread of democracy rise. It's the freedoms to vote and to be voted for, to express oneself and join the bandwagon of choice, to access the free press and the ballot box, that give democracy its verve. The right to stand for election, once a pipe dream for many, has now been bumped up to the status of a universal human right.

The history of voting rights is a bit like a well-constructed drama, with enough twists and turns to keep the audience hooked. Initially, the voting club was as exclusive as an aristocratic tea party, with only the well-heeled having an invite. Over the years, the guest list expanded to include all grown men, then women, and eventually every Tom, Dick, and Harriet of voting age, irrespective of their colour, gender, or wallet size. In the U.S., amendments 15 and 19 ensured African American men and all women respectively could join the voting jamboree.

Universal suffrage, where every adult citizen has the right to vote, is now seen as a standard feature of democracy's package deal. But like all packages, there are terms and conditions. Some restrictions are considered as necessary evils for the greater good, like not letting the young ones vote due to their perceived lack of worldly wisdom.

Some democracies even give certain individuals the boot from their voting rights. In parts of the U.S., felons get a double whammy — not only do they lose their freedom, but they also lose their vote too. It's a contentious issue, with debates still raging about its fairness and how it skews the democratic representation.

Then there's the curious case of compulsory voting, as seen in nations like Australia and Belgium. It might seem like a slap on the face of freedom, but they argue it's for a noble cause – to boost voter turnout and keep extremists from capitalizing on voter apathy.

Freedom of expression, association, and a free media are the salt, pepper, and oregano that give the democracy stew its flavour. Just look at the Nordic countries like Denmark and Sweden, who keep these freedoms close to their hearts and routinely rank high on democracy hit parades.

Access to the ballot box is democracy's non-negotiable. In India, the democracy heavyweight, the Election Commission moves heaven and earth to ensure that every citizen, even those tucked away in the remotest corners, gets their vote. Democracy goes the extra mile, sometimes literally, to uphold this freedom.

In a nutshell, freedom is not just a brick in the wall of democracy; it's the whole darn building. Strip democracy of the freedom to elect and be elected, to speak one's mind, to freely associate, to access an unshackled media and the ballot box, and you're left with a hollow shell. Some restrictions might pass muster, but they should be rare sightings, not regular features. Democracies need to be perpetual freedom fighters, upholding, protecting, and amplifying these freedoms.

The rule of law

Imagine if democracy and the rule of law were flatmates. In the best-case scenario, they'd be more than just sharing a pot of coffee and squabbling over cleaning duties. They'd be utterly symbiotic - the sort of flatmates who finish each other's sentences and seem to thrive off each other's presence. In fact, they're so indispensable to each other; it's near impossible to think about one without the other.

Democracy is that well-intentioned chap who believes in equality, freedom, and justice for all. But lofty ideals are tricky to put into practice. And that's where his flatmate, rule of law, comes in. He's the meticulous one who ensures that everyone - yes, even the bigwigs running the show - behaves in a way that's deemed acceptable.

An exceptional democracy, the sort that turns

heads and wins hearts, cannot exist without its flatmate. Rule of law is the unsung hero, the custodian of political rights, civil liberties, and accountability, the guy who makes sure that democracy isn't just about equality in theory, but also in practice. He's the one who ensures that power, no matter how intoxicating, isn't misused.

But what makes this flatmate tick? He's a stickler for three rules: First, law reigns supreme, and it's the same set of rules for everyone - no exceptions. Second, no one gets a get-out-of-jail-free card - not even those running the country. And finally, everyone gets a fair shot at justice. Together, these principles keep the spirit of democracy alive, safe from the tentacles of government overreach.

Remove rule of law, and the democracy starts to crumble like a half-baked cake. Political rights and civil liberties take a hit, and the whole system begins to look rather shaky. Case in point: North Korea, Zimbabwe, and Venezuela. Here, power abuse and disregard for law run amok, reducing democracies to shadows of their former selves. An independent judiciary is conspicuously absent, and corruption, the unwelcome guest, hampers the enforcement of laws, leading to grievous rights violations.

A good flatmate, rule of law is a champion of fair play. He insists on free and fair elections and sets the guidelines for politicians. Without him, democratic processes are open to foul play. He's also the one who makes sure the government is kept on its toes, safeguarding free press and independent oversight bodies from falling prey to power abuse.

He's the torchbearer of civil liberties. With him around, citizens can voice their opinions, assemble freely, and join hands to stand up for their interests. Without him, as seen in countries with severe censorship and assembly restrictions, the democratic process is effectively choked, curtailing citizen participation in governance.

In essence, the flatmates - democracy and the rule of law - are inseparable. If they maintain a healthy relationship, democracy flourishes. But without the rule of law, democracies risk sliding into chaos. So, it's crucial that all democracies out there take good care of the rule of law, preserving political rights, civil liberties, and accountability mechanisms, thereby ensuring political equality, and checking potential abuses of power.

Separation of powers

Democracy, like a well-designed skyscraper, depends on the strength of its pillars to avoid collapsing under its own weight. Separation of powers - that's your primary load-bearing pillar. This characteristic, as essential to a healthy democracy as greens are to a balanced diet, divides government responsibilities into separate branches to avoid a power monopoly. These branches — legislative, executive, and judicial — perform a sophisticated ballet, forming a system of checks and balances to guard democratic principles like a watchdog and fend off potential abuses of power.

Think of the legislative branch, often a parliament or congress, as the master chef, concocting the laws that govern the state. The executive, the president or prime minister, or the monarch if you're still into the old school, is the server, presenting and enforcing these laws. Lastly, the judicial branch, the courts, and the judges, are the critics, interpreting the laws and settling disputes under them. This respectful independence of each branch is the secret ingredient in the recipe for a well-functioning democracy.

Let's take a trip to the dark side for a moment: a concentration of power. Imagine one entity or individual hoarding all the power - it's like watching your favorite character transform into a villain, suffocating democracy. The wise old Aristotle, sounding alarm bells centuries ago, warned us that single entities holding legislative, executive, and judicial powers are the birthplaces of despotism.

Thank goodness, then, for the separation of powers, our democracy's secret weapon, establishing a system of checks and balances. Each branch has the ability to monitor and influence the actions of the others, ensuring they behave. The US, for example, gives the president (executive) veto powers, but Congress (legislative) can still override this with a two-thirds majority vote. The Supreme Court (judicial) possesses the power of judicial review, effectively the right to tell laws or executive actions to take a hike if they're unconstitutional.

Meanwhile, in the UK, the Prime Minister

(executive) may suggest laws, but it's Parliament's (legislative) job to give them the thumbs up. And the judiciary, though it doesn't hold the same 'judicial review' superpower as its US counterpart, keeps the legality and constitutionality of other branches' actions under a sharp microscope.

The true elegance of this system lies in the friction it purposely produces. This friction, sparked by the constant scrutinizing of each branch by its siblings, breathes life into a healthy democracy. It catalyses debate, demands compromise, and throws a speed bump in front of hasty decisions, lowering the chance of arbitrary or autocratic rule.

Separation of powers also hands us a golden ticket to accountability. When power is split, each branch can be held responsible for its actions as its functions are clear and conspicuous. This visibility allows us, the public, to pinpoint who to cheer or jeer for specific governmental actions, thus encouraging responsible governance.

In the final analysis, separation of powers is the heart and soul of democratic systems. Distributing power across different branches and creating a system of checks and balances acts as a safety catch, ensuring no single entity becomes the Hulk. It cultivates robust democratic debate, reinforces accountability, and safeguards citizens' rights and liberties. It's the robust framework within which democracy flexes its muscles, ensuring that power truly emanates from the people, belongs to the people, and serves the people.

Universal vote

Universal suffrage is much like a staple diet of fruits and veggies – crucial for health, yet alone it won't get you in Olympic shape. Democracy, too, needs more than just the right to vote to blossom into its full potential. It must be nurtured by factors like political enlightenment, enthusiastic participation, and the prevailing social landscape.

Let's mull over the 'Wise Men vs. People' debate, which has been causing quite a ruckus in the voting discourse. Critics are quick to whip out their spectacles and point to an uninformed public making dodgy choices. Yet, this argument shimmies into treacherous territory. Who, pray tell, do we deem the 'wise men'? Tricky, isn't it?

We might inadvertently sideline swathes of the population, neglecting democracy's heart — equal say for all. Remember the old war cry, "No Taxation Without Representation"? There's a reason it didn't fade into obscurity. It's a firm reminder that each citizen, regardless of their wisdom score, has a stake in society and warrants a say in steering its course.

On the topic of voting rights, the status of non-nationals is hotly disputed. Sure, they may not hold citizenship, but they still kneel before the law, use public services, and cough up taxes in their resident country. To bar them from voting could translate into substantial chunks of the populace going voiceless. Conversely, we mustn't turn a blind eye to the concern of divided loyalties, especially in the scenarios of dual-citizenship or religious affiliations. The challenge lies in walking the tightrope. Countries like New Zealand and Denmark have offered a compromise, letting foreigners vote in local elections where they're directly affected.

The debate on the voting age is a similar can of worms. While 18 is generally accepted, some dare to propose a reduction, given the palpable effect political decisions have on young'uns. Critics, however, furrow their brows at the maturity and political savvy of such budding voters. It's a sticky wicket, ensuring representation without sabotaging the quality of democratic choices.

And let's not forget, the health of democracy isn't merely about who gets the voting card, but who bothers to use it. Voter turnout is the pulse of democracy, reflecting citizen engagement and trust. A weak pulse can signify large, ignored sectors of the population. Some nations, Australia, and Belgium, for example, have attempted resuscitation by enforcing compulsory voting, reviving voter participation. Yet, critics argue it smacks of coercion and infringes on individual liberty.

The elixir to a thriving democracy, then, doesn't lie solely in handing out voting rights like candies, but in enhancing the democratic ambiance. Political education, engagement-driving initiatives, and a commitment to equal representation can ensure the universal vote is more than just a feel-good theory but a potent tool of democratic participation.

For instance, initiatives like voter education programs could be the silver bullet against the 'wise men' argument, equipping citizens to make informed choices. Likewise, mechanisms ensuring transparency and accountability could breed trust in the system, perhaps coaxing out more voters on Election Day.

To wrap it up, universal suffrage is a keystone of democratic architecture. But it's no magic cure-all for democratic woes nor an independent support pillar. It's a part of the larger democratic jigsaw puzzle that appreciates and fosters political enlightenment, equal representation, active participation, and safeguarding of fundamental rights. Only then can the universal vote meaningfully contribute to a democracy worth writing home about.

The military and democracy

The relationship between the military and democracy is akin to the delicate dance between fire and ice — a balancing act of power that needs constant vigilance. Within a democratic framework, the use of force is the privilege of the military but is wielded under the watchful eye of civilian power – a construct often referred to as the liberal democratic model of civil-military interaction. The model imagines an idyllic world with professional armed forces respecting the rule of civilian authority. Mercenaries may be employed, though generally considered undesirable, primarily due to their allegiance tied to financial gain rather than national interest.

Democracy, in its essence, demands a two-fold accountability – the armed forces must fall under the purview of civilian control, and the civilian custodians must submit to the democratic process. In simpler terms, the men and women who pull the strings need to be watched too.

However, like a jigsaw puzzle with pieces constantly morphing, the reality isn't always so straightforward. The question invariably arises – does the military, the machinery with a monopoly over legitimate violence, have an inherent predisposition towards dictatorships?

To unravel this query, let's dive into some historical contexts. The military in Latin America, particularly during the 1970s and 1980s, was notoriously known for its alignment with autocratic regimes. Countries like Argentina, Brazil, and Chile witnessed military juntas overthrowing democratically elected governments, subsequently ushering in brutal dictatorships. In these scenarios, the military not only became the government but also served as the machinery of repression, fostering widespread human rights violations.

Conversely, in more recent times, we see military institutions supporting transitions to democracy, notably in countries such as Tunisia following the Arab Spring in 2011. Here, the military's refusal to support the autocratic regime played a pivotal role in the transition to a more democratic system.

Drawing broad conclusions from these examples is risky, given the unique socio-political landscapes of each country. However, it provides some insight into the dual character of the military in the context of political power – sometimes the guardian of democracy, at other times its gravedigger.

The path to maintaining a harmonious relationship between the military and democracy lies in a carefully maintained equilibrium. An independent, professional military that respects civilian authority is crucial. Equally important is the commitment to democratic values by those civilians who wield power over the military and police.

The military's allegiance should ultimately lie with the nation and its constitutional mandate, rather than with specific political parties or ideologies. Its focus should be on defending the nation from external threats, leaving domestic policing and power transitions to civilian institutions. Meanwhile, the civilian authority must exercise its control judiciously, involving the military only when necessary and ensuring its professional autonomy.

Moreover, democracies must invest in building strong, accountable civilian institutions and fostering a culture of democratic governance. Transparency, accountability, and respect for human rights should be non-negotiable elements in both civilian and military spheres.

In conclusion, while the military, with its power to enforce and ability to disrupt, has the potential to be a stumbling block for democracies, it can also serve as a significant pillar supporting democratic structures. The trick lies in maintaining the balance – ensuring the military's professional autonomy while upholding civilian control, all under the umbrella of democratic governance. It's a delicate dance, indeed, but one that's vital for the health of any democracy.

Majority rule and the rights of minorities

If we were to think of democracy as a grand orchestral symphony, then the principle of majority rule would be the principal violinist. However, for the symphony to truly captivate, every instrument - or in our case, every facet of the democratic system - must harmonise, each playing its part to create a resonant whole.

Just as a symphony needs its conductor, democracy requires accountability and transparency. The elected officials, our conductors, are not there to rule but to serve. Their every decision and action must be made under the scrutiny of the public's critical gaze, the ultimate critic of our metaphorical concert.

Yet, left to its own devices, democracy can hit

a sour note, evolving into a majority tyranny that tramples on minority rights. Here, we turn to our trusty constitutional safeguards. Like the music stand to a violinist, they provide the support and stability that prevent our system from collapsing into cacophony.

But let's face it, even the best symphonies have their shaky moments. Low accountability and reduced citizen participation can lead to a wobbly performance. The stage becomes skewed, allowing activist minorities like LGBT+ groups and secret societies like Masonry to hog the limelight and potentially exert an influence larger than their fan base. Achieving the right pitch here is a tricky task, but there are ways to fine-tune the balance.

We can liken laws protecting minority rights to the sheet music in front of our musicians. They guide and regulate the melody, ensuring that every note, i.e., citizen, plays an equal and fair part in the performance. For instance, the Civil Rights Act in the United States makes certain that no note is silenced due to race, color, religion, sex, or national origin.

Then there are the constitutional limits on the power of the majority. They're akin to the conductor's baton, keeping the symphony's tempo and making sure no instrument drowns out the others. The judiciary, like a discerning music critic, steps in if these limits are overstepped, protecting the integrity of the symphony.

Now, think of a representative democracy as our orchestra pit. Within it, each voice, or in our case, each societal group, finds a place. A system like proportional representation ensures that every instrument - big or small - gets its solo, its chance to shine.

Let's not forget the vital role of our audience, the civil society. They are the ones clapping, booing, demanding encores, and thus keeping the performers - the elected officials - in check. The louder the applause or the boos, the more in tune the performance is with the audience's tastes.

And what is an orchestra without its musicians? The more participants, the richer the sound. High participation rates prevent one or two instruments from dominating the concert and create a more varied, complex performance. Making it easier for musicians to join the orchestra, or citizens to vote, adds depth to our democratic symphony.

In summary, while the principal violinist of majority rule might lead the democratic symphony, it must be carefully orchestrated by constitutional limits that protect the entire ensemble and give every musician a solo. Keeping our orchestra in tune - balancing majority power with minority rights, promoting accountability, transparency, and wide-spread participation - is a tough gig. But it's all worth it when the symphony that is democracy plays not just for the majority, but for all. Now that's a performance worth an encore.

Democracy and impeachment

Democracy is like a communal bicycle ride through the labyrinth of governance. We hop on, vote in a tour guide, and hope they possess a sturdy sense of direction, steering clear of potholes and ditches. But what if the guide starts pedaling towards a precipice or, worse, circles aimlessly? Enter impeachment, the emergency brake that stops the bicycle from veering off into chaos.

Historically, impeachment dates back to 14th-century England when the "Good Parliament" essentially said, "Baron Latimer, you're taking the mickey!" The U.S. took this concept and cycled with it — their Constitution allows for impeachment based on "treason, bribery, or other high crimes and misdemeanors." In contrast, Britain's egalitarian approach means that any elected official can stand trial for crimes.

Impeachment is a democracy's airbag. It's a safeguard, not a dramatic coup d'état or revolution. However, akin to a potent detergent, misuse or overuse can damage the fabric of democracy. In countries like Brazil and the US, we've seen it employed as a political scoreboard, compromising its intent.

Now, let's imagine the captain of our democratic bicycle is someone like Donald Trump. When does the shaking handlebar indicate it's time to hit the brakes? Mental unfitness? Treason? Like discerning between minor pebbles and hazardous boulders on our path, the decision to impeach must be weighty and justifiable. We don't deploy airbags for a pebble, nor should impeachment be invoked for frivolities.

However, democracy's very essence is tested when it becomes a puppet show for demagogues, kleptocrats, or people whose decision-making might be influenced by a tweet they just read. Sometimes it becomes evident that democracy needs safeguarding from itself. When there is a genuine threat to the democratic structure, like a case of extreme illness, heinous crimes, or subversion of democratic institutions, impeachment becomes a necessary evil.

In the cacophony of political clamor, we must tread carefully. Is mental unfitness grounds for impeachment? A cautionary tale here - history is replete with slightly off-kilter leaders who still managed to not run their countries into the ground. However, with today's geopolitical scenario, an unhinged leader could be a proverbial child playing with a loaded gun - especially with nuclear codes.

Treason, on the other hand, is unambiguous high grounds for impeachment. However, a mere affinity for dictators or failure to disclose tax returns doesn't necessarily meet the treason benchmark. The big guns of impeachment need to be saved for clear and present dangers to democracy itself.

Equally important is the due process. Impeachment is like picking a lock – you only do it when absolutely necessary and not because you don't fancy using your keys. The process must be transparent, with an independent review, so it doesn't morph into a political weapon. The decision should involve other elected officials, an attorney general, and ultimately rest with an independent judiciary.

Moreover, an intriguing proposition is whether an aggregation of borderline reasons could be grounds for impeachment. Here, we tread in uncharted waters. The concentration of such decisive power in one entity can be likened to putting all your eggs in a potentially fickle basket.

In conclusion, impeachment is an invaluable safety mechanism within a democracy, akin to the emergency brakes on our communal bicycle. But it is imperative that this tool be employed judiciously, backed by substantial reasons and following a thorough due process. We must ensure that it serves as a last resort to protect the integrity of the democratic process and not as a bludgeon in the arsenal of political manoeuvring. Democracy, after all, is a delicate balance, and its airbags.

Politicians' accountability

In our ever-intriguing game of democracy, politicians are rather like poker players holding the nation's hand, and we the voting public, keen spectators. This raises the question: should politicians, those powerful card players, be held accountable through mere voting or should they face the justice system too, civil, or criminal?

Take Portugal's recent debate over their former Prime Minister, José Sócrates. His leadership led to a crushing electoral defeat and his subsequent resignation from the Socialist Party. Is this enough or should he and his trusty aides face the firing squad of prosecution?

There's a reason the more sophisticated democracies tend towards political accountability: it prevents the triumphant politicians from vengefully making the losers walk the plank, or blaming all future mishaps on the inheritance from their predecessors. Otherwise, we're knee-deep in a tit-for-tat political soap opera reminiscent of coup-laden African states.

Now, let's not throw out all reason. For crimes like pocketing public funds or indulging in some sweet corruption, by all means, let's extend accountability to the courts. But to decide fiscal responsibility of public funds? What court is qualified to judge that, and by what standards?

And what about doling out penalties for poor decisions? Shall we ask Minister Teixeira dos Santos to cough up the 4 billion Euros that the BPN nationalisation cost or slap a hefty fine on Minister Manuel Pinho for his costly affair with subsidising EDP Renováveis and other wind energy producers? And who's to judge the direct responsibility? Is it the Prime Minister or the Council of Ministers? And the cost-benefit assessment of these decisions is always a hotbed of controversy.

So, it's a merry go round of questions. But while we ponder over them, let's not forget, it's our politicians playing the cards.

In the grand theatre of failed projects, it's quite a spectacle when we can pinpoint the villain of the piece with certainty (our favourite duo, Tribolet and Zorrinho in the technological fiasco, for instance). But in most acts, responsibility is a shared treasure, scattered across several governments and their departments. The uncontrollable Public-Private Partnerships, health sector spending, New Opportunities, agricultural and vocational training support – a veritable buffet of waste away. Such a sprawl makes any judicial proceedings a clear exercise in futility.

So, instead of dragging these culprits through the courts or waiting for the hand of justice dealt by the voting public, allow me to propose a rather unconventional approach. Let's pen down the "Black Book of Public Wastefulness of the Last 20 Years". A tome meticulously crafted by an "independent commission of sages" for the future memory and benefit of generations to come. In its pages, we'd list the chief perpetrators, both direct and indirect, of public fund squandering, along with an evaluation of the harm caused and their motivations, justifications, and negligence. A little keepsake to remind us of how not to run a government.

82

3 The Various Types of Democracy

Democracy, a multifaceted concept of governance by the people, encompasses diverse forms worldwide. In this exploration, we delve into the rich tapestry of democratic systems that have shaped history and continue to shape our present and future.

At its core, democracy embraces representation, empowering elected officials to make decisions on behalf of the people. We uncover the mechanisms and ideals of representative democracy, illuminating its ability to give citizens a voice and protect their interests.

As we sashay gingerly into the untamed jungle of democracy, with its twisting vines and overgrown theories, let's take a moment to ponder. Representative democracy, that grand old dame, might have hogged the limelight, but behind the curtain lies a kaleidoscope of understudies, eager to show off their fancy footwork.

Within representative democracy, we encounter two prominent models: parliamentary and presidential systems. Each possesses distinct intricacies and dynamics, shaping the course of governance through the interplay between executive and legislative branches.

Then, we'll contrast "Hereditary vs. Republican Regimes". We've got royalty with a family business in ruling, versus republics that prefer election over birthright. Their takes on democracy? As different as chalk and cheese

Democracy strives to reflect the popular will, but the delicate balance between majority rule and preserving individual rights poses a paradox. We confront the challenges of 'popular democracy,' where the power of the majority can overshadow minority rights, seeking to reconcile popular sentiment with principles of inclusivity and justice.

Plebiscites, referendums, and direct votes occasionally feature in democratic systems, allowing direct citizen participation. We investigate the implications and potential pitfalls of direct forms of democracy, exploring opportunities for engagement alongside risks tied to simplified decision-making.

The remnants of fallen dictators cast long shadows on the path to democracy. Reflecting on the challenges faced by transitioning nations, we explore the legacies of fallen evil dictators and their lasting impact on democratic processes. Historical narratives provide insights into the struggles, triumphs, and ongoing dilemmas societies encounter on their democratic journeys.

Navigating the democratic landscape, we encounter the intricate complexities of the European Union—an experiment in regional democratic governance. Unraveling the balance of power, accountability, and representation within this framework, we explore how the European democratic model interacts with the diverse traditions and complexities of member states.

As if that's not enough excitement for one chapter, we'll waltz into the cheeky tango between multinationals and states, where money does the talking and modern feudalism is the name of the dance. And, just when you thought the show was over, out come the predators lurking behind civilization, gnashing their teeth at the fragile democratic ideals like overzealous fans at a rock concert.

Join us on this enlightening journey as we explore the various types of democracy, encompassing representative, parliamentary, and presidential systems, as well as hereditary regimes and republican models. We examine the potential of plebiscite democracy, dissect the European Union's democratic experiment, and contemplate the challenges posed by transitioning from dictatorial rule. Together, let us unravel the intricate threads that weave the tapestry of democracy, gaining a deeper appreciation for its diverse and intricate nature.

True democracy is representative democracy

Let's talk about "Los Indignados". Now, before you roll your eyes and label it just another teen tantrum, hear me out. This sit-in, happening in Madrid and other European capitals, is not your typical "we're young, loud, and want to rule the world" type protest. It's not about trying on a new trendy rebellion, like swapping skinny jeans for bell-bottoms. No, it's more profound than that.

Sure, each generation enjoys its ritual of standing up to the old guard. The latest trends, new bands, fringe political views - these are all part of the rite of passage. And despite the odd scuffle sparked by the thrill-seekers among them, it's mostly harmless fun that gives the world some color.

But let's not confuse youthful exuberance with the issues at the heart of the Indignados movement. These young folks aren't annoyed just because they can be. They're miffed about broken dreams and the frightening specter of unemployment. They've grown tired of politicians who seem more adept at crafting empty promises than delivering hope.

Naturally, fringe political groups, from the traditionally left-leaning to anarchists, have tried to fish in these troubled waters. And ironically, that's precisely why many youths steer clear of these protests - no one likes to be used as a pawn in someone else's game. Yet the core of the Indignados is led by honest-to-goodness, non-partisan leaders.

So, why are we still hearing echoes of revolutionary utopias and anti-capitalist mantras in their cries? Maybe it's easier to grasp onto radical slogans when you feel the system has failed you. But here's the crux of the issue. Some protesters are demanding "Real Democracy Now through neighborhood assemblies," essentially promoting direct democracy, which, historically, has proven as reliable as a chocolate teapot when it comes to providing actual democracy.

This clamor for 'direct rule by the people' smacks of populism and seems rooted in a romantic but flawed view of ancient Greek democracy. Real democracy, the kind that doesn't unravel at the first sign of trouble, is representative democracy. It's where the majority rule, but within a framework that ensures the minority don't get their rights trampled on.

So, while Los Indignados might have some genuine gripes, they need to remember that democracy isn't a game of instant gratification. It's a long, arduous ride that requires compromise, representation, and, most importantly, patience.

To Our Youth: Demanding Democracy, Capitalism, and a Dose of Patience. So, our young rebels are scratching their heads, asking why their elected representatives seem as concerned with their worries as a cat with a dog's life. They're looking for answers: Is it because these representatives couldn't care less? Is it because their hands are tied? Or is it that they believe the stormy labor market will soon see sunny days again? Or, even worse, are they preaching that their actions will eventually bear fruit, but like a slow cooker, it'll take some time?

Well, firstly, we've got to bust that myth. Elected officials are not cold-hearted creatures. And secondly, they need to tackle the bogeyman that's driving these young ones up the wall — uncertainty.

Our classic liberal progressive politicians can't just sit back, expecting the young to go through some anger therapy, courtesy of our left-wing revolutionaries, and wait for their anxiety to miraculously evaporate. Telling a youngster who's been twiddling their thumbs on the unemployment line for two years that the market will one day wave a magic wand and fix everything, is like telling a kid that Santa will bring them a pony.

What they need is hope. And they need it pronto. So, whether our politicians put their faith in demand or supply measures, they need to show they're doing something. And they need to do it now.

But it's not enough to just act. They also need to roll up their sleeves and explain why representative democracy, coupled with constitutional liberalism and market capitalism, is not the enemy. They're not some evil triad conspiring to ruin their future. Quite the contrary, they're the best chance of ensuring these youngsters have a future to look forward to.

So, here's the deal. Democracy, capitalism, and constitutional liberalism are the solution, not the problem. They're the key to the treasure chest of hope. But the catch is, they work on their own timetable, not ours. They require understanding, faith, and most of all, a bit of patience.

Failed alternatives

As we navigate through the wild winds of democracy, it's hardly surprising that the ship often springs a few leaks. Complaints about the system have become as regular as the change of seasons. But don't be fooled. The case against democracy remains as thin as a wafer biscuit at a Weight Watchers meeting, despite the authoritarian peacocks fluffing up their feathers on the world stage.

Take China's charming claim that a communist dictatorship sprinkled with a dose of capitalism is the recipe for economic success. It's like saying that combining vinegar and milk makes for a palatable drink. On closer inspection, it curdles. China's impressive growth figures have often been earned at the cost of social and environmental harmony, and the personal freedoms that many of us take as casually as a cup of tea in the morning are non-existent.

Then there's the seductive allure of plebiscite democracy, which has been strutting its stuff in Switzerland quite successfully, making the rest of us look like wallflowers at the democratic disco. However, the sweet success of Switzerland is far from universal. Despite the promises of online remote voting that seem to crack open the door to a wider application of plebiscite democracy, no one else has been able to walk through it. And why not? Well, it seems that letting everyone have their say on every issue, at every moment, is as practical as wearing a chocolate teapot.

Now, I hear you ask, if these alternatives don't do the trick, what's left? Here's the crux of the matter – lurking behind all these models is an unsavoury truth about our nature, as unavoidable as a hangover after a night of wild abandon. We humans have an innate predatory instinct, something civilization has worked tirelessly to tame, like trying to teach a cat not to chase a mouse.

Civilization, in its great wisdom, has nudged us towards systems that curb this instinct. Representative democracy is one such system, one that acknowledges our flaws but finds a workable way around them. In this delicate dance, citizens entrust their leaders with the responsibility of decision-making, while retaining the right to boot them out if they fail to deliver. It's a bit like hiring a gardener and then keeping a keen eye on the roses.

Yes, representative democracy can sometimes seem as efficient as a sloth on sedatives, and its tendency towards bureaucracy as infuriating as a satnav that sends you down a dead end. But when compared to the alternatives, its strengths become evident. It provides a framework for a society where personal freedom is possible, where varied voices can be heard, and where power is not the exclusive privilege of a chosen few.

So, before we throw the democratic baby out with the bathwater in our quest for an elusive perfect system, let's consider this: while democracy may be slow, messy, and frustratingly imperfect, it's a system that, despite its shortcomings, continues to hold the predatory side of our nature in check, allowing civilization to thrive. In the grand pageant of governance, that's not a bad track record. In fact, I'd say it's as good as it gets.

Parliamentary vs presidential democracy

The democratic riddle revolves around the age-old question - who holds the power? While the answer is deceptively simple (the people, of course!), the ways this power is expressed and managed can be as varied as our morning coffee orders. Today, we shine the spotlight on the two heavyweights of democratic systems - parliamentary and presidential - and take a no-nonsense dive into their structures, strengths, and snags.

Picture the parliamentary democracy as a rather cosy dinner party. The guests, or legislative members, pick out one of their own to play host and lead the evening. The host, also known as the prime minister, basks in the glow of democratic legitimacy, served hot by the legislative branch. Countries such as the United Kingdom, Canada, and Germany are proud members of this club.

The parliamentary system is like an expressway for legislation. With the executive and legislative branches intertwined like a pair of ballet dancers, laws pirouette their way from inception to enactment with relative ease. This system also has the handy feature of being able to show the door to a prime minister who oversteps, via a parliamentary vote of no confidence.

However, every party has its party-poopers. Parliamentary democracies can shun minority views and lack the crisp separation of powers, raising eyebrows over unchecked rule.

Now, let's hop across the pond to the presidential democracy, where the executive and legislative branches enjoy their space like flatmates with clearly marked shelves in the refrigerator. The head of state, the president, is directly elected by the people, serving a set term. The United States and Brazil are poster children for this system.

The presidential system flaunts a clear division of powers like a prized heirloom, preventing power hogging and providing checks and balances. The direct election of the president also offers a tangible sense of democratic responsibility.

Yet, this system isn't immune to hiccups. It's vulnerable to legislative standoffs, creating policy-making speed bumps when different parties control the executive and legislative branches. Plus, the president's fixed term might seem like a stint in a straitjacket, potentially keeping an ineffective leader in power till the next electoral dance.

Then there is also the option of a mixed system in countries like Portugal or France. In the real world, it's not a one-size-fits-all scenario. The success of each system is like a jigsaw puzzle, with pieces like political culture, societal norms, and historical nuances fitting together. The UK's parliamentary system has been a rock of stability, while Italy has seen a revolving door of governments. Across the Atlantic, the US's presidential system has maintained a healthy separation of powers but also witnessed legislative stalemates, a la the Obama era's Republican Congressional roadblocks.

To sum up, parliamentary and presidential democracies, much like morning coffee orders, have their distinct flavours. The choice between them often mirrors a nation's history, ethos, and social fabric. Whether they choose a parliamentary flat white or a presidential espresso, the ultimate goal for any democratic nation is to foster freedom, equality, and rule of law while effectively addressing its citizens' needs and dreams.

Hereditary vs republican regimes

Crowns or Ballot Boxes: The Game of Thrones in the Real World. Democracy, that glorified and well-embraced child of the 21st century, has settled snugly into the hearts and minds of global citizens. Even so, a couple of old-fashioned relatives persist in the family portrait - the hereditary and republican regimes, each flashing their peculiar smiles.

Hereditary rule, or monarchy, is a bit like inheriting grandma's antique silver: it's all about lineage. Power gets passed down family lines like a precious heirloom. Republican regimes, though, are the opposite - they're the bustling flea markets of the political world, where power is picked up by the people and their elected chums. Strangely enough, these contrasting relatives can share the same democratic living room, provided the division of house chores - or power, in this case - is well-managed.

Take our old friend, the United Kingdom. It's a bit of a hybrid beast, combining a constitutional monarchy and a parliamentary system. The monarchy is hereditary, but it's mostly there for show and tell, like the portraits of old relatives on the mantle. The real hustle and bustle occur in the parliament, where democracy gets to flex its muscles. This quirky blend lets the UK have its royal cake and eat it too - preserving a sense of continuity and national identity, while also ensuring democratic rule.

In the corner painted in blue, white, and red, we have France, a stalwart of the republican regime. The French have made a national sport of electing their president, emphasizing the power of the people. It's a system that strives to embody 'égalité' and 'fraternité', making sure that anyone, regardless of their origins, can have a shot at the top spot.

However, we must not get carried away by the labels on the tin. Both hereditary and republican systems are simply the scaffolding of the political building. The democratic substance within the structure is what really matters.

Consider Saudi Arabia, a monarchy by nature, but hardly a democracy in practice. The reigning monarch wields uncontested power, making it a stark contrast to democratic ideals. And then there's Syria - a republic in name, but under substantial scrutiny for not exactly playing by the democratic rulebook. Clearly, this type of regime doesn't always reflect the level of democracy.

As we shuffle the deck of hereditary and republican regimes, it is important to remember that neither guarantees a democracy jackpot. What counts are the democratic aces - people's participation, free speech, rule of law, human rights, and transparent governance. These aces can turn up in a monarchy or a republic - it is all in how the game is played.

So, are we better off with crowns or ballot boxes? Often, the answer is as varied as the historical, cultural, and societal landscapes in which they exist. Each system has its trump cards and wild cards. The true winning hand, however, lies in the steadfast adherence to democratic values that champion the rights and freedoms of citizens. Whether it is the UK or France, what we learn is that democracy is not a rigid rulebook, but a dynamic game that adapts to its context. After all, as in any game, it's not just about the cards you're dealt, but how you play your hand.

The paradox of 'popular democracy'

In the wild rumpus of political conversation, the term 'popular democracy' leaps out like a charming rogue: by the people, for the people, power handed to the people on a silver platter. It struts about, dazzling in its democratic purity, purporting to be the embodiment of our collective desires. Yet, when you scratch beneath the surface, peeking into history's musty corners—be it the French Revolution or various communist experiments—one finds an uncomfortable truth: popular democracy can be as popular as a wet Monday and about as democratic as a mob boss.

Take the French Revolution for instance, a time that turned heads with its enticing mantra of "Liberty, Equality, Fraternity." Billed as a glorious overthrow of monarchy and the birth of people's rule, it promised the moon and then some. But just as the champagne bubbles burst, the

Revolution slipped into a gruesome Reign of Terror. Radical upstarts, armed with the veneer of popular democracy, led a dictatorship that made the worst school bullies look like choir boys. The so-called 'people' ended up cowering under the iron fist of the likes of Robespierre, not holding power as the brochure promised.

Fast-forward to the 20th century and communism fancied a fling with popular democracy. Marxism-Leninism, for example, flirted with the 'dictatorship of the proletariat,' a concept that in theory would have democracy buffs swooning. But the reality was as romantic as a cold shower. Be it in the icy chill of Soviet Russia or amid the sweeping landscapes of Mao's China, these regimes morphed into autocracies. Power pooled in the hands of a select few, while the majority of the populace didn't get a look in.

The nub of this paradox lies in the presumption that the will of the people is as uniform as a row of tin soldiers, ready to be marshalled by a single, authoritative voice. But societies aren't made from cookie cutters; they're a bustling bazaar of ideas, interests, and values.

From the Parisian streets to Soviet squares,

concentrating power in a central authority has consistently led to stifling dissent and pushing minority views to the periphery. What starts as a seemingly noble quest for collective good soon transforms into a monstrous tyranny, squashing any opposition in the name of the 'popular will'.

What's more, the pillar of popular democracy, direct rule by all, can often be as practical as a chocolate teapot. Building consensus on every issue among a diverse population is a logistical nightmare, vulnerable to the machinations of those silver-tongued charlatans who can manipulate public sentiment. The fear of 'tyranny of the majority' is not just academic musings, but a real concern, where the rule of the most can slip into outright dictatorship.

To top it all off, the romance with popular democracy tends to brush aside the importance of institutions and checks and balances, the unseen superheroes of a functioning democracy. Without these safety nets, the journey from people's will to people's despotism is frighteningly short, as the haunting tales of Robespierre's France and Stalin's Soviet Union testify.

To wrap it all up, the weight of history tips the

scales against popular democracy. It can often abandon its democratic ideals, revealing the dangerous liaison between people's will and people's rule, which can quickly descend into authoritarian rule.

Take North Korea, for instance. The constitution makes it sound like a democratic utopia, a "dictatorship of people's democracy". Sounds like the people rule the roost, right? Not quite. Picture a place with almost no political freedom, where human rights are merely decorative terms, and transparency is as rare as a hen's teeth. Doesn't quite scream 'democracy', does it?

Then we have the aftermath of World War II. Eastern European countries like Poland, Hungary, Romania, you name it, rushed to adopt this shiny new model, 'People's Democracies'. They claimed it was a stepping stone to socialism, where the state rules the economy, and only one party gets to play. But with the Communist Party's iron grip and dissent treated like a disease, their 'democracy' card started to look a bit dog-eared.

Leftist movements in Latin America have been pulling the same trick, labeling regimes in

Venezuela or Nicaragua as 'popular democracies'. But when you peel back the layers, you find the familiar stench of authoritarianism – concentration of power, undermined judiciary, suppressed opposition, and elections manipulated like a rigged card game. It's like a 'democracy' painted on a crumbling wall.

What's with this misdirection? It seems we're confusing 'popularity' with 'populism'. A democratic system needs to reflect the people's will, sure, but popularity – especially the type you whip up with stirring speeches – doesn't automatically mean you're playing fair. This sleight of hand helps autocratic leaders wrap their rule in the cloak of the people's mandate.

Here's the thing: real popular democracy is about more than just 'majority rules'. It's about freedoms like speaking your mind, assembling peaceably, having an independent judiciary, a lively civil society, and a government you can hold to account. If a regime snuffs out these liberties in the name of 'popular democracy', it's like selling you a Rolex in a back alley – it just doesn't add up.

So, what's the take-home message? 'Popular democracy' sounds great in theory, but often masks the grim face of authoritarianism in practice. It's crucial to tell the difference between lip service to democracy and the real deal, because a true popular democracy isn't just about ruling by the majority, it's about guarding everyone's rights and freedoms. Now, wouldn't that be a real slice of the democratic cake?

Plebiscite democracy

Now the whole purpose of having a representative is not to be bothered all the time with questions. However, how can one resist the allure of a plebiscite democracy, a glittering showstopper on the world stage? Switzerland, in all its direct democratic glory, has been shaking its tail feathers at the democratic disco, making the rest of us feel like shy wallflowers. But let's not be fooled by the sequinned suit of plebiscite democracy, for beneath its flashy veneer lies a caveat: one size does not fit all.

Plebiscite democracy seems to be working just dandy in Switzerland. In fact, it's such a hit there, you'd think it was the fondue of political systems. Online remote voting seems to be the cherry on top, promising to fling open the doors to a widespread adoption of this form of governance. But, alas, the sweet promises have remained just that - promises. As it turns out, others haven't quite managed to cut a rug in the democratic disco as Switzerland has.

But why? Isn't direct democracy supposed to be the solution to our political woes, the cure to our democratic hangover? You'd think it would be as easy as popping a couple of aspirin and watching our democratic headache dissipate. Well, not quite.

Letting every citizen have a say on every issue, at every moment, is as practical as trying to pour a piping hot cup of tea from a chocolate teapot. A delightful thought, indeed, but rather messy in practice. Imagine that scene for a moment — steaming liquid poured into delicate china, only for the teapot to melt, and the tea to mingle with molten chocolate. A disaster for your tea, your tablecloth, and your sanity.

The fact is, we can't all be Switzerland. Just as not every country can produce world-class chocolate or impeccable watches, not every nation can pull off plebiscite democracy. It might work beautifully in a compact, relatively homogeneous society, but in a sprawling, diverse nation, it might be as jarring as a poorly tuned cuckoo clock.

Our technological advances are like a double-edged sword; they promise to ease the way to plebiscite democracy, but at the same time, they threaten to oversimplify complex issues. Online polls and the like may seem an obvious route to increased democratic engagement, but what they offer in accessibility, they often sacrifice in nuance.

Let's face it, a tweet-sized opinion, tapped out on a smartphone screen, might not capture the complexity of an issue the same way a thoughtful essay or a lively debate might. Picture trying to squeeze the works of Tolstoy into a text message. Doesn't quite work, does it?

Moreover, the dangers of plebiscite democracy aren't just logistical; they're societal too. In an era of polarising online echo chambers and increasingly adversarial political discourse, the last thing we need is more fuel for the fire.

So, as tempting as it is to join the democratic disco, perhaps it's time for us to redefine the dance. Perhaps it's not about matching

Switzerland's moves, but creating our own. For every country, like every dancer, has its rhythm, its style. And perhaps it's time we realised that a chocolate teapot, however impractical, can be quite delicious if enjoyed in the right way. Plebiscite democracy is no different - it may not be everyone's cup of tea, but when it works, it's a sweet dance to behold.

Democracy and fallen evil dictators

The gruesome end of Kaddafi resurfaces a dilemma: how should advocates of democracy deal with monstrous dictators? Such tyrants, often burdened by paranoia, commit crimes in a variety of scenarios: 1) engaging in war atrocities against foreign nations, 2) resorting to extreme violence in domestic civil wars, and 3) ruthlessly persecuting and starving their own citizens.

Measuring a dictator's level of brutality often boils down to tallying the death count outside the battle arena. For instance, while the body count from Napoleon's cruelties in Portugal was significant, it pales in comparison to battlefield deaths. Conversely, the fatalities caused by the Red Army during China's civil war were fewer than those who perished from hunger and persecution under Mao Tse Tung during the infamous "Great Leap Forward" and "Cultural Revolution." Consequently, Mao is often categorized among the deadliest dictators, rubbing shoulders with the likes of Hitler, Stalin, and Pol Pot.

Of course, not all dictators meet the same fate as Kaddafi. Some, like Mao, Pol Pot, and Kim Il-sung, die peacefully and continue to be worshipped by their followers or descendants. Others, like Hitler, opt for suicide before capture. A few escape or are exiled, as happened with Napoleon and Idi Amin. A tiny fraction face domestic or international tribunal, with outcomes ranging from capital punishment (as with Saddam Hussein) to lengthy imprisonment.

Ideally, in democracies that abhor the death penalty, long-term imprisonment should be the norm. Such a course of action would not only exemplify the superiority of democratic justice, but also serve as a deterrent and a lesson. However, a handful of dictators have met such an end.

The preference for eliminating defeated tyrants is typically driven by vengeance or the fear of their return, neither of which are democratic virtues.

If Kaddafi had been handed over to the

International Criminal Court, his trial could have unearthed valuable insights into how he corrupted numerous regimes worldwide. For the sake of transparency, it's crucial that NATO and Libya's new leadership conduct thorough investigations into why he wasn't preserved alive and held accountable in a court of law.

A Brussels twist: A dash of dickens

Where there's smoke, there's fire – and in the EU's case, a good dose of smog. The persistent coughing fit is due to a thorny issue: representation. When one meanders through the maze-like hallways of EU's governance, two things spring up like some strange flora: direct representation via the European Parliament, and indirect representation through the European Council, a patchwork quilt of government representatives. Yet, many Europeans feel like the proverbial Oliver Twist, crying out for more from an unfeeling Brussels dispensary. A remedy for this representation blues may just lie in splitting the European Parliament into two – a lower house directly elected, and an upper house stocked with members of national parliaments. A smidgen of the US Congress here, a dash of the UK's Houses of Parliament there, and voila! We might have an enhanced EU democracy recipe.

Take the United States Congress, for instance. It's a snappy two-in-one package: the House of Representatives, directly chosen by the people, embodying the essence of democratic representation, and the Senate, with its state equality ensured by two senators apiece, balancing diverse regional interests. It's democracy served with a generous side of equilibrium.

The UK's parliamentary system is a similar dish, albeit with a different garnish. The House of Commons, voted in directly by the public, and the House of Lords, a non-elected entity playing the parts of critic and polisher. The Lords might raise a few eyebrows with their unelected status, but their role in fine-tuning legislation and providing expertise generally meets with a nod of respect.

Now, transplant this bicameral model into the EU body and it could serve as a vitamin shot to its democratic health, and help shed the image of Brussels as a faceless, indifferent entity. The lower house would carry on the role of the current European Parliament, singing the song of EU citizens and setting the democratic rhythm. Meanwhile, the upper chamber, brimming with representatives from national parliaments, would provide the much-needed bass line, syncing Brussels with the heartbeat of national politics across member states.

This new upper chamber would not only be a political round table for national parliaments, but it would also strike a chord between pan-European and national interests. Representatives could croon about their constituents' concerns, adding a layer of relatability to the polyphonic EU policy composition. This musical bridge might just make Brussels seem less like a distant concert hall and more like a local jamming session.

The proposed upper chamber could also sharpen the EU's policy and legislative notes, much like the House of Lords in the UK. This fine-tuning could enhance the harmony of the EU's legislation, ensuring it hits all the right notes before being played to the public.

However, let's not dance to the tune just yet. With such a reform comes challenges. Structural overhauls demand a chorus of agreement among member states, and sorting out details like representative allocation and the upper chamber's exact responsibilities would need careful conducting. We certainly wouldn't want to hit a sour note by creating a bloated bureaucratic orchestra.

In the final refrain, the idea of a 'two-chamber' European Parliament strikes an interesting chord for better EU representation. By orchestrating a symphony of direct and indirect representation, this setup could amplify the democratic melodies of the EU, making it more attuned to its citizens' voices and better equipped to handle the orchestra of interests within its concert hall. Despite the dissonant notes inherent in any reform, the potential for a harmonious democratic symphony makes it a score worth perfecting.

Multinationals, state, and democracy

Remember the Middle Ages, when lords and serfs were all the rage? No? Me neither. But we've all read enough history to know that feudalism and democracy are chalk and cheese. Today, though, some smarty pants are arguing that our shiny democracies are sliding backwards into a kind of neo-feudalism. The idea is that there's a merry-go-round of top dogs from big business, media, and government, all hopping from one seat to another. And with the cost of election campaigns spiraling upwards like a rocket, these cashed-up elites are the only ones left in the running.

Over in the United States, it's like a reality show – "Big Business meets Politics." The rising cost of campaigning leaves only those with the deepest pockets, often from corporations or who have their own, in the race. As the boundary between corporate might and political leadership becomes as blurred as my vision after two glasses of wine, democracy starts to look more like a feudal system, with economic powerhouses pulling the strings.

But with big money comes big competition, like a high-stakes poker game. Look at the Koch brothers, once proud donors to Trump's campaign, only to flip and fund the opposition. Then there's Elon Musk, who started off waving the Democratic flag, then surprised us all by buying Twitter, reportedly to prop up right-wing candidates and perhaps even cheer for foreign strongmen like Putin.

This scene of battling billionaires is less 'democracy in action' and more 'Game of Thrones.' It's starting to feel like our shiny democracy is morphing into a glitzy neo-feudalism, where the loaded and powerful control the levers of power. So, where does that leave the rule of the people, by the people, for the people?

Sure, there's a chorus calling for limits on campaign spending, hoping it might derail this neo-feudal express. But with the rise of social media and public affairs agencies, there are more ways than ever to spend money and more holes for foreign interference to sneak through. Policing campaign financing in today's digital world is like trying to catch smoke with a butterfly net.

And even if we do limit campaign spending, it's not like it magically removes the influence of the wealthy from politics. Corporations and billionaires have other tricks up their sleeves — lobbying, media manipulation, strategic investments, you name it. It's a tangled web of politics, money, and power. So, are we in a democratic crisis?

That's the million-dollar question. Or should I say billion-dollar question? The rise of billionaire-politicians and corporate influence undeniably shifts power from the many to the few, reminiscent of feudal times. But let's not write off democracy just yet. It's been around the block, weathered storms, and adapted, always clinging to its vital principle - power to the people.

In conclusion, the shadows of a neo-feudal order looming over modern democracies certainly raise eyebrows. The encroachment of corporate interests on political leadership threatens the bedrock of democratic governance. While capping campaign spending may be a piece of the puzzle, we need a broader solution - tougher regulations, transparency, and citizens ready to roll up their sleeves. After all, we need to make sure democracy stays afloat in this stormy sea and remains, as Lincoln put it, "of the people, by the people, and for the people".

4 About Power and Collective Decisions

In the labyrinth of human society, power, and decision-making form the scaffolding that undergirds the course of civilization. This chapter, "About Power and Collective Decisions," embarks on an exploration of these deeply entrenched notions, dissecting their complexities, and shedding light on their influences that stretch from the corridors of political offices to the confines of our living rooms.

Our journey begins with an analysis of "The Lust for Power", a phenomenon as old as humanity itself. We dive into the psychology and motivations behind individuals' relentless pursuit of influence and authority, seeking to uncover the intricate tangle of desire and ambition that breeds this lust.

We then turn to the "Sources of Power: Force vs. Ideas vs. Interests". This section delves into the diverse origins of power, breaking it down into its constitutive elements: the overt strength of force, the transformative potential of ideas, and the hidden leverage of interests. By dissecting the root causes of power, we aim to shed light on the mechanisms behind its acquisition, consolidation, and exertion.

In the section "Decision Theory and Democracy," we bridge the gap between mathematical theories and political realities. Democracy, as a system that leverages collective decisions, is dissected through the lens of decision theory, enabling us to understand the processes that underpin it and the challenges inherent within.

After we reach "Merit or Mediocrity: Democracy's Dilemma". In this section, we grapple with one of democracy's most persistent paradoxes — the balance between electing competent leaders (meritocracy) and representing the masses (mediocrity). It's a complex, often contradictory dynamic that continues to shape the face of democracies around the globe.

In "Power Worshippers" we explore the role played by those willing to serve under any political system or to become turncoats with the prevailing wind. In this context we examine Hungary and Poland, the bold pioneers in kicking out communism, but have now done a U-turn.

Followed by two examples from Portugal in Regime's End and The Portuguese Experience and the Arab Spring.

Finally, in "Voting as Selection and Sanctioning" we explore the mechanics of collective decision-making. We investigate the pivotal role voting plays not just as an instrument for electing leaders, but also as a tool for citizens to express approval or disapproval of those in power, thereby acting as a form of societal check and balance.

This chapter promises a multifaceted exploration of power and collective decision-making, probing their nuances and complexities. Through this discourse, we hope to not only enrich your understanding of these concepts but also inspire you to think critically about their roles and manifestations in our society.

The lust for power

Now, listen here. I'm about to take you on a bit of a wild ride through the shadowy, intoxicating world of power and how we, as humans, seem to have an insatiable craving for it. You know the kind I mean: power, the ultimate aphrodisiac; authority, the ultimate high; influence, the ultimate currency. It's a phenomenon as old as the first caveman who discovered he could get others to gather his berries if he was a big enough bully.

Human psychology, it seems, has been hard-wired for power lust from the very beginning. It's in the fabric of our DNA, bound up with survival and the survival of our genes. It's survival of the fittest, the meanest, the slyest, in its most Machiavellian form. We crave power because, at a primitive level, it helps us survive and thrive, from the playground to the boardroom, from the tribe to the nation.

Now, here's the rub. Democracy, bless its heart, tries to put a rein on this power-lusting beast inside us. The idea is that power should be alternated, shared, lost, and won again, all in an orderly fashion. But oh, how this must chafe at our primal instincts! That's like asking the alpha wolf to step down every few years and let the omega wolf have a go. It goes against the grain of everything our power-loving hearts desire.

But then, along comes John Maynard Keynes, the economist, with his rather clever twist on things. He had the bright idea that perhaps we can channel our lust for power into something less harmful — our wallets. Tyrannize over our bank accounts, not our fellow countrymen, he said. A sort of economic power as a substitute for political power, if you like. Now, isn't that a fascinating idea?

Let's not kid ourselves, though. Money is power. It's a different kind of power, perhaps, but it's still power. You can't tell me the man with the billion-dollar bank account doesn't hold sway over the man who's living from paycheck to paycheck. Is it a safer form of power, this economic might? Is it less likely to corrupt, to seduce, to lead us into all sorts of mischief?

Who can say? I do know this, though: the lust for power, be it economic or political, is a part of who we are. It's woven into our history, our psychology, our society. It's a part of our very humanity, for better or for worse. We can try to temper it, to channel it, to direct it toward better ends, but it's not going away any time soon. It's a dance as old as time, and we're all stumbling along, trying not to step on each other's toes.

Sources of power: force vs ideas vs. interests

Ladies and gents, power is a sly, slippery creature. It slithers and slides around, sometimes right in front of our faces in the form of brute force. Other times, it's a little more subtle, working its magic through the catalyst of groundbreaking ideas. And then, there are the times when it's so cunning, it's practically invisible, pulling the strings from behind the scenes through the leverage of vested interests.

Let's have a look at these characters, shall we? First off, the undisputed heavyweight champion of power sources: brute force. Force is the bulldog of power, the muscle that struts its stuff in the broad daylight for all to see. It's there in the sharp end of a spear, the report of a gunshot, the growl of a tank. It's in the clenched fist, the steel-toed boot, the raised voice. It's the oldest, most primitive source of power, as crude as it is effective.

Then we have the dark horse of the power world: ideas. Now, ideas are a funny thing. They don't seem like much. You can't touch them, you can't see them, but oh boy, can they change the world. The power of an idea lies in its ability to worm its way into people's minds, to shape their views, to influence their actions. They are the tools of philosophers and revolutionaries, of dreamers and disrupters. An idea, as Victor Hugo said, is a force once it has seized the masses.

Enter Albert Hirschman and his beautifully complex book, "The Passions and the Interests". He delves into the idea of how economic interests could act as a check on the destructive passions of humans. A powerful idea, that, transforming how we think about economics and its role in society.

And then we have the shadow puppeteers of power: interests. Hidden, quiet, but always present. Interests work behind the scenes, influencing decisions, guiding actions, shaping policies. They are the unseen hands that turn the wheels of power, often under the guise of 'public good' or 'national interest'. But whose interests are we talking about here? That, my friends, is the million-dollar question.

Keynes famously quipped that "practical men, who believe themselves to be quite exempt from any intellectual influence, are usually the slaves of some defunct economist." A perfect encapsulation of the stealthy power of ideas and interests. For in reality, those practical men, those movers and shakers of the world, are often dancing to the tune of long-dead economists and the subtle drumbeat of vested interests.

So there you have it, the three musketeers of power: force, ideas, and interests. Different faces, different methods, but all with the same goal: to control, to influence, to hold sway. They are the puppet masters behind the stage of life, pulling the strings, making us dance. Understanding them is the first step to recognizing how power operates in our world. And who knows, maybe even learning a few dance steps of our own.

Decision theory and democracy

Alright folks, hold onto your hats, because we're about to dive into the dizzying world where mathematics and politics intersect. It's a fascinating place, filled with strange creatures like random selection, structured sampling, neural networks, and other exotic tools from decision theory. The question is, can these mathematical beasts help us better understand and improve our democratic processes?

Democracy, at its core, is all about collective decision-making. We come together, air our views, and make choices about who should lead us and how we should be governed. It's a messy, noisy, often frustrating process, but it's ours. It's the bedrock upon which our society is built.

Enter decision theory, a branch of mathematics that deals with the best ways to make choices. It's all about probabilities, expected outcomes, and optimizing decisions based on available information. It's a world of precision, clarity, and cold, hard numbers.

So, can these two worlds meet? Can the pristine logic of decision theory help us navigate the muddy waters of democratic decision-making? Could we, for example, use random selection to ensure a truly representative sample of the population? Or structured sampling to ensure all voices are heard? Could options theory help us make better choices? Could neural networks help us predict and understand voting patterns?

There's a certain allure to the idea. Imagine a democracy turbo-charged by mathematics, a system where every decision is optimal, every choice the best possible one. Imagine a world where our leaders are chosen not by vague impressions and media spin, but by precise, data-driven processes.

But here's the rub. Democracy isn't just about making optimal decisions. It's about people, with all their passions, interests, and ideals. It's about the noisy, messy, gloriously unpredictable business of human interaction. Can a mathematical model capture the fire of a political debate, the fervor of a campaign rally, the quiet determination of a voter in the booth? Can an algorithm understand the subtle play of interests, the shifting alliances, the sudden swings of public opinion?

Perhaps not yet, but who knows about the

future? As our tools grow more sophisticated, as our data grows more comprehensive, who's to say we can't build a model that captures the essence of our democratic process? A model that doesn't replace human decision-making but enhances it, sharpens it, makes it more effective.

But until that day comes, let's not forget the human element in our democracy. Let's not lose sight of the passions, the interests, the ideals that drive us. For it's these very qualities that make our democracy vibrant, robust, and truly representative. So, by all means, let's embrace the tools of decision theory. Let's use them to refine and improve our processes. But let's not forget that at the heart of our democracy is not an equation or an algorithm, but the beating heart of the people.

Merit or Mediocrity: Democracy's Dilemma

Ah, the age-old debate: does representative democracy yield a government of sparkling merit or mind-numbing mediocrity? The answer, my friends, is about as clear as mud.

When we pop our vote into the ballot box, we don't always opt for the glittering paragons of excellence. More often than not, we choose a motley crew of politicians, a quirky blend of those who champion merit and those who wave the flag of ideology.

But hold on, let's not be too hasty in our lamentations. This mixed bag might be the saving grace of our society. Because if history has taught us anything, it's that entrusting government to an assembly of so-called 'technical experts' doesn't necessarily produce a utopian society. Quite the contrary, it can be as risky as juggling eggs on a trampoline.

Authoritarian regimes, ranging from Bismarck's Germany to Brezhnev's Soviet Union, have gambled on this approach, hoping that technocrats, econocrats, and bureaucrats, armed with their specialist knowledge, could steer the ship of state to safer shores. These regimes assumed that those at the helm were consumed by the quest for efficiency, guided by their 'problem-solution' mindsets, rather than by any vested interests. But alas, the ship often crashed against the rocks.

This fascination with efficiency – the means – often clouds the vision of the ends. It's a slippery slope, my friends, where we start believing that the end justifies the means, and that's a rabbit hole no one wants to tumble down.

Take the horrific example of the engineers behind the gas chambers in the Nazi concentration camps. They may have crafted an efficient death machine, but the moral enormity of their actions was overlooked, hidden behind the flimsy excuse of "just following orders".

The flavour of the month in terms of which professional class should rule the roost might change with the seasons – one minute it's the engineers, the next the economists, then the lawyers, scientists, doctors, media professionals, and so on. But the core issue remains sticky as a treacle.

A system that crowns leaders based on merit under equal opportunities is indeed a beautiful notion, as long as it doesn't result in a self-contained elite class looking down their noses at the rest of us.

So, let's put a fresh spin on an old adage: politics is too important to be left solely to the 'experts'. Our democracy needs a varied menu, not just the daily special, because in this ever-evolving world, diversity – not homogeneity – is the secret sauce to success.

Power worshippers

Have you ever had the sense of looking at something so bizarre, it defies logic? That's precisely what's happening in Eastern Europe. Picture this: Hungary and Poland, the bold pioneers in kicking out communism for a more democratic approach, have now done a U-turn so dramatic it would give a gymnast whiplash. They've traded democracy for what looks suspiciously like proto-fascism.

This disturbing trend is insightfully dissected by Anne Applebaum in her riveting book, "The Twilight of Democracy." She talks of how friendships forged in the furnace of early democratic struggle dissolved like sugar in hot tea. The reasons for this sugar rush? A potent cocktail of demagoguery and nostalgia, it seems.

In the spirit of openness - something I've always rated - let me weave in a thread of my own experience. I've seen firsthand how political chameleons, whether of the right or left hue, change color. It's either because they didn't get the revolutionary goodies they were eyeing, or the siren call of power, no matter the bearer, is simply irresistible.

In 1974, Portugal's left-wing coup offered a fantastic study in political behavior. Some of the ousted lot bent the knee to their new masters, while others reinvented themselves as radical leftists, outdoing the new rulers in zeal. The successful ones morphed into such skilled sycophants that they could have taught the old regime a lesson or two.

Zoom forward to 1993 in Budapest, and you'd have seen me nosing around some banks. I couldn't help but notice a tepid welcome for the new foreign owners from bankers who seemed to think that success came from political handshakes rather than entrepreneurial nous. Their disgruntlement found an outlet in a turn to nationalism, as convenient as it was predictable.

Fast forward to 2002, in my academic playground, I decided it was time to swing the pendulum away from our radical left-wing image. But, oh dear! The moment I hung up my Dean's hat, my former cheerleaders started giving me a wide berth. Amusingly enough, after a few rounds of this avoid-the-Dean game, I found it easier to engage with my old rivals than with these fair-weather friends.

So, here's the punchline: The art of the political flip-flop isn't exclusive to the left or the right. The real motivation? A power grab, pure and simple. Take the budding politicos in Hungary or Poland. They've clocked how Russian oligarchs have lined their pockets through politics rather than through business savvy, and are more than a tad miffed that democracy doesn't serve up wealth quite so easily.

That, dear reader, is the silver lining to this tale. Democracy, for all its flaws, keeps a check on those power worshippers. Now that's something to hold on to.

Regime's end: Stories from Portugal

The recent bungled attempt by loyalists of Prime Minister Sócrates to wrestle control of the Portuguese media is so grotesque, it's practically reminiscent of those unhinged final acts of regimes gasping their last breaths. Take for instance, Sócrates managing to plant two of his cronies as executive directors in a hefty company where the State has barely chipped in a dime. It's almost as absurd as when Emperor Caligula, in a madcap move, appointed his beloved horse to the office of consul in the heyday of the Roman Empire. The question, my dear readers, isn't about when Sócrates will hit the exit, be it tomorrow, three years, or seven down the line.

What truly intrigues us is whether the impending cycle will be a mere rerun of the three post-April 25 episodes I've had the, ahem, pleasure of witnessing, or if it will usher in a seismic shift in Portuguese society. Regrettably, the pervading pessimism and dearth of fresh ideas have set my expectations at a dismal low. But let's not paint the future too grim. Positive change may still be lurking around the corner.

For instance, I recall a day in March 1974, as I was ambling out of the ISE (now ISEG) via the Miguel Lupi gate. I overheard a military man (a general, perhaps?), a neighbour, remark that the Caldas coup had come a cropper. The day before, I'd watched a rally on TV showcasing a veritable who's who of rheumatic old gents pledging allegiance to Prime Minister Professor Marcelo Caetano. It filled me with a heavy sense of foreboding, and I could hardly envisage myself marching towards the Estádio Primeiro de Maio, brimming with euphoria and utopian dreams of a shiny post-April 25 Portugal.

A few months spent in the thick of the trade union movement, however, was an eye-opener. I realised that human nature, when propelled solely by the thirst for retribution against the excesses of a toppled regime, has a nasty habit of coming full circle. Yesterday's victims transform into today's tormentors. The only reliable safeguards against such a vicious cycle are robust systems of representative democracy and constitutional liberalism.

Back in the fall of '85, huddled in the Solneve da Covilhã hotel, nervously awaiting the PRD vote results that eventually exceeded our expectations, hope was the guest of honour. The newfound party was heralded as the knight in shining armour, destined to not only lay the ghosts of PREC to rest but also pioneer a new era of political ethics. However, reality, being the ever-unyielding tutor, had a second lesson in human nature waiting in the wings. It's not enough to lambaste the void of ethical values if we have no viable alternatives to offer, values anchored in equal opportunities and personal freedom, drawing inspiration from Enlightenment ideals. I was oblivious to the fact that a new era of economic expansion, led by a public works-driven boom (colloquially referred to as 'Cavaquismo'), was about to dawn.

Fast forward to 1995, as I kept a watchful eye

on the emerging socialist cycle from my London perch, I viewed it as a mere hiccup in the Cavaquista era. Indeed, when I returned in 1998, somewhat seasoned and more conservative, I flirted briefly with the idea of re-engaging in active politics. This fleeting thought was promptly snuffed out when Marcelo Rebelo de Sousa relinquished his post as PSD leader, giving way to a swarm of idea-starved, career-lacking ex-Jotas. Politics, to these Jotas, was a mere stepping stone, a ticket to a lucrative career they neither attempted nor were equipped to build via the time-honoured tradition of hard work and diligent study.

Whether the present cycle is the dying breath or one of the final chapters of the state-capitalist experiment of the Third Republic, dominated by socialist and social democratic ideologies, is immaterial. What is crucial is ensuring this cycle doesn't simply give way to a rehashed version of state capitalism, irrespective of whether it leans to the left, right, or oozes oligarchic or mafioso tendencies.

After the tumultuous century following the French invasions, and more than 80 years under the yoke of state capitalism post the First Republic, it's high time for Portugal to close this less than glorious chapter of its recent history. A different future can only genuinely be built on a new regime, one underpinned by representative democracy, one of the six pillars of human happiness that forms the leitmotif of my blog.

Portuguese experience and the Arab spring

In the spring of 1974, Portugal found itself in the throes of a peaceful uprising that came to be affectionately known as the "carnation revolution". A merry band of young military officers instigated a coup d'état that overthrew Salazar's rather stale authoritarian regime which had reigned since 1928. A scant two years later, Portugal emerged as a democracy, serving as the poster child for peaceful regime changes led by the people – notably inspiring Eastern Europe. But can this Portuguese experience shed light on the Arab Spring and pave the way for peaceful democratic transitions in the Arab world? Let's unpack the luggage of similarities and differences.

Our Portugal of yesteryears was a peculiar mix: secular yet profoundly Catholic, with the Church standing firmly by the side of the old regime. It was a land taken aback by the revolution, devoid of political parties, save for the clandestine communist party. Yet Portugal was a NATO member, albeit teetering on the edge of a communist takeover for two years. Western allies chipped in, fostering the birth of new democratic parties, and warning the Soviets not to rerun their Eastern European playbook in Portugal. The potential catastrophe? Trading a pro-western authoritarian regime for an anti-western communist dictatorship.

Similarly, with the Arab uprisings, the nightmare scenario is swapping pro-western authoritarian regimes for anti-western theocratic dictatorships. Should then Western nations back a Portuguese-style makeover in the Arab world?

Weighing the odds, they seem rather dicey, especially with the specters of Pakistan and Iran in mind. Yet, when viewed alongside Portugal, the stakes appear even more colossal. Let's consider the military. While the armed forces in many Arab countries also sport Western training, they're neither tied to a democratic military alliance like NATO nor are they immune to the allure of corruption, unlike their counterparts under Salazar. In matters of religion, a stark contrast unfolds. After enduring centuries of wars, Catholicism had loosened its grip on the political reins. Yet, Islam, in stark contrast, holds considerable sway. Moreover, there's no overarching leadership akin to the Soviet Union to keep in check within the Islamic sphere.

Crucially, Portugal was a cultural and social appendage of democratic Europe. Regrettably, such an atmosphere is elusive among Arab and Muslim nations. Of the 50+ countries with Muslim majorities, less than a third are secular. Only two flaunt a democratic tag (Malaysia and Turkey), but alas, none are Arab. So, as we mull over the Portuguese experience, we must tread carefully through the nuanced terrain of the Arab world.

If we're placing bets on the emergence of a peaceful democratic switcheroo, it's safe to say the odds are painfully slim. The rather unsavoury prospect of an anti-western theocratic dictatorship seems to be peeking around the corner, and we must be well-stocked with a plan B, especially if it flexes its military muscles menacingly. Let's be clear - democracy isn't some off-the-rack suit that can be forced onto anyone. The Arab people hold the reins of their destiny, and it's up to them to decide when to cozy up with democracy. The tricky bit? They may need to loosen religion's chokehold on politics first.

That said, the West isn't obliged to paint all dictatorships with the same brush. The three dictatorial breeds - theocratic, monarchic, and military - display varying degrees of regard for peace and human rights.

In this befuddling maze, I'd be the first to hoist the white flag of joy if our pessimism is proven misplaced. So, here's to hoping against hope.

Voting as selection and sanctioning

Now, I'd like to talk about something we all take for granted, a little nugget of power we hold in the palms of our hands: the vote. It seems such a mundane thing, a minor blip in our busy lives. We nip into the local school or community centre, make a few scribbles on a piece of paper, and pop it into a box. But, my dear reader, that little act is no trivial matter. It's a weapon, a tool, a bargaining chip in the game of democracy. It's a way to pat our leaders on the back or give them a swift kick in the pants.

Let's have a closer look at this voting business. At its most basic, it's a selection process, a sort of democratic beauty contest. We parade our potential leaders on a stage, they strut their stuff, and we get to decide who wears the crown. It's a simple, efficient way of picking who gets to rule the roost.

But there's more to it than that. Voting is also about sanctioning. It's not just about choosing our leaders; it's about keeping them in line. Our votes are the rewards we dangle before them and the stick we brandish behind them. Do well by us, and you get another term. Fail us, and it's out you go.

The beauty of it is voting is the civilized answer to conflict and social unrest. Instead of settling our differences with guns and bombs, we use ballots and boxes. It's a system based on mutual advantage, a delicate dance of give-and-take. It's an acknowledgment that it's better for all of us if we work together, even when we don't always agree.

But here's the catch. For this dance to work, everyone needs to play by the rules. There's always the temptation to sit back, let others do the work, and reap the benefits. The so-called free riders. Then there are the stubborn ones, the recalcitrant, who refuse to fall in line, disrupting the rhythm of our democratic dance.

That's where our little nugget of power comes in. Our votes become the means to enforce the rules of the game. They become the means to reward the diligent and punish the freeloaders.

They become the means to encourage cooperation and discourage disruption.

Of course, it's not a perfect system. There are flaws, hiccups, and the occasional misstep. But consider the alternative. A world without voting is a world where power lies solely in the hands of the strong, the wealthy, the influential. It's a world where the average Joe has no say, no influence, no power. It's a world I, for one, would rather not live in.

So, let's cherish our votes, my friends. Let's wield them wisely, responsibly, assertively. Let's use them to reward and punish, to select and sanction, to encourage and deter. For in our hands, that little piece of paper isn't just a vote. It's a declaration, a stand, a shout into the void that we, the people, have the power. And we're not afraid to use it.

5 On Representation

Dear beloved readers, put your thinking caps on and brace yourselves for a roller coaster ride through the scintillating landscape of representation. If you thought representation is just a bland affair of proportionality, then, my dear friends, you are in for a treat. We will venture into the thrilling depths and dissect the splendid creature that representation is. Oh, and we'll do this with the verve and wit worthy of a detective on the hunt!

In the section "Representation is not the same as proportionality," we will dust off the old school assumptions and illuminate how representation is more than just a numbers game.

But wait, there's more. "Universal Representation vs. limited representation" will unfurl the tantalizing contrast between a representation where everyone gets a golden ticket, and one where access is as restricted as an exclusive, invitation-only soirée.

And just when you think you've seen it all, behold "Representation by random selection." We'll take a page from ancient Athens and explore the intriguing possibilities of letting fate decide who gets to rule.

Now, don't even get me started on "Political Parties and Representative Democracy". This is where the rubber meets the road, folks. We delve into how these beloved and often despised clubs play matchmaker in the marriage between representation and democracy.

Fasten your seat belts as "The Anatomy of Power Inside Political Parties" takes you on a wild safari, exploring the intriguing inner workings of the powerhouses we call political parties.

In "Be Aware of Party Youths" a word of caution about nepotism and the dangers of inbreeding among politicians, with special emphasis on Portugal.

Lastly, like the grand finale of a spectacular show, "How to reduce the power of the establishment" guides you through the exhilarating, audacious, and sometimes devious ways of Direct Election of Party Leaders.

REPRESENTATIVE DEMOCRACY

Representation is not proportionality.

Why should we, the public, pass the baton of power to a handful of elected representatives? Simple, we believe this select group can do a superior job at governing than if we attempted to wrestle with every political decision ourselves.

Now, imagine a world where voters are categorised into countless distinct identities - based on gender, age, ethnicity, ancestry, physical attributes, literacy levels, religious beliefs, honesty, sexual orientation, IQ, and a laundry list of personal traits. Should each of these groupings, then, have the right to elect their representatives? This, my friends, borders on the ludicrous. Not only can we carve out infinite identity groups, but the crucial point is, we all wear multiple hats, and our identities aren't always indicative of our governing abilities or our qualifications for the job at hand.

This is precisely why representation should be granted to those we deem as like-minded and most qualified for the task, typically through open party organisations.

But here's the rub. What if these parties morph into impregnable fortresses dominated by self-perpetuating special interest groups, or 'partocracies', that sideline or discourage certain identities (say women or the Roma community)? The answer is simple. Don't vote for such parties.

But what if some parties, without overt discrimination, fail to tap into the talent pool across various identity groups (e.g., retirees, the youth, Jews, immigrants, etc.)? Should voters still shun these parties? Not necessarily, if voters are not in favour of positive discrimination, or they believe certain identity groups simply do not wish to dive into the political arena.

This underscores why positive discrimination policies should never be enshrined in electoral rules. The onus lies with the parties to put these policies into action, and the voters to evaluate their efficacy.

Yet, we are at an inflection point, where the very essence of democracy is under threat. Parties have shifted their focus from championing their ideologies and ideals, to claiming representation of specific identity groups (e.g., championing the cause of businesspeople rather than market capitalism, or LGBT+ communities over sexual freedom).

Instead of engaging in a battle of policies, parties have adopted a divide-and-conquer strategy, segmenting the electorate into as many identities (electoral tribes, if you will) as possible, which they purport to represent.

This brings us to the crux of the matter. Proportionality is ushering in a new wave of tribalism and is a menace to authentic representation. Taken to its extreme, this focus on identity politics can potentially sound the death knell for democracy.

Universal vs. limited representation

The universal right to elect and be elected is, undoubtedly, an intrinsic part of democratic ethos. But we must pose a pertinent question: Does this unrestricted access inherently lead to the effective workings of our democracy? The American bicameral system offers us a valuable case study on systems of representation, where the House of Representatives extols the virtues of universal representation, whereas the Senate serves as a sanctuary for limited representation.

Today, universal representation has clearly taken centre stage. But if we put this under a microscope, has there truly been a significant shift from the hereditary confines of the 19th century? Sadly, the evidence points to a rather disheartening 'no'.

You see, the establishment, once infiltrated, shuts its doors tightly and morphs into an impenetrable fortress. A prime example can be found in contemporary US politics. Who could have imagined that the Republican party would remain steadfastly under Trump's influence, with each successive candidate seemingly striving to outdo his notorious bad legacy? The likes of DeSantis and Greene, and others of their ilk, seem to make Trump look mild in comparison. Meanwhile, figures such as Liz Cheney find themselves in the wilderness, their appeals for reason and sanity falling on deaf ears.

This leads us to a rather alarming question. How can we prevent the lunatics from taking over the asylum, so to speak? Can we institute some sort of 'fit and proper' test to assess suitability for political office?

I must confess, I don't have a ready answer. However, what's evident is the dire need for solutions. The survival and health of representative democracy hinge on addressing these challenges.

On one hand, universal representation allows for a broader cross-section of society to participate in governance. It creates a more inclusive platform where people from diverse backgrounds can bring their unique perspectives to bear on decision-making processes.

On the flip side, limited representation—curtailing the pool of electable individuals based on specific criteria—can lead to a more experienced, qualified set of representatives. These individuals may bring with them a wealth of knowledge and understanding, making them better equipped to navigate the complex terrain of public service.

Yet, the dichotomy between universal and limited representation isn't as clear-cut as it seems.

Universal representation, in theory, democratises the political process, but in reality, can be hijacked by powerful, self-perpetuating establishments. Limited representation, meanwhile, could create an elitist system, inaccessible to many, but it also has the potential to ensure competent, qualified governance.

As we grapple with these complexities, what becomes clear is that the discourse surrounding representation must evolve. We need to consider new paradigms and innovative solutions that address the twin challenges of inclusivity and quality in representation, ensuring the continued vitality of our democracies. After all, democracy's strength lies in its adaptability, its ability to respond and evolve with societal changes. And it's high time our ideas of representation did just that.

Representation by random selection

It's undeniable that the principle of "one person, one vote" forms the bedrock of any functioning democracy. Entrusting the decision-making power to elected representatives is a tried-and-tested mechanism. Yet, in an era where disenchantment with career politicians is increasingly commonplace, one can't help but wonder: could there be a more efficient way to choose our representatives? Could the potential solution lie in random selection?

Consider the justice system, where we rely on juries, randomly selected from the populace, to deliberate on matters as grave as life and death. We trust these everyday citizens to reach decisions of profound importance, guided by the expertise of legal professionals. If such a system is not just functional, but accepted and respected, could a similar model work for our political representation?

The concept might seem radical at first blush, but perhaps it isn't as far-fetched as it seems. This model would see our representatives selected randomly from the general populace, much like a jury. These representatives would then be supported by a cadre of experienced civil servants, the political equivalent of the legal professionals guiding a jury.

Is such a system of representation both feasible and desirable? That's the million-dollar question.

Random selection, also known as sortition, was, after all, the cornerstone of Athenian democracy. It's also been successfully employed in modern citizen assemblies to deliberate on key issues such as climate change and constitutional reform. The logic is simple: a truly random sample is more likely to be a microcosm of society, representing a diversity of perspectives and experiences that a traditionally elected body might not. It could diminish the influence of powerful interest groups and reduce corruption.

That being said, we must be mindful of potential pitfalls. Random selection might not always result in competent, qualified governance. It also doesn't guarantee active participation or informed decision-making and could lead to a lack of accountability. After all, a randomly selected representative would not be beholden to an electorate.

The proposal of random selection isn't a call to abandon our current systems of electoral representation wholesale. It's a suggestion to stir up debate, to challenge the norms, and to think creatively about how we might revitalize our democracies.

In the end, it's not about replacing one system with another, but about enriching our democratic practices. Imagine a political landscape where electoral and sortition-based systems work in tandem. Elected politicians could be balanced by randomly selected citizen assemblies, providing a check and enriching policy debates with their diverse perspectives.

The idea of random selection as a complement to our current democratic practices isn't just radical, it's radically democratic. It demands that we see every citizen not just as a voter, but as a potential representative, capable of shaping the policy landscape.

In this age of democratic discontent, perhaps it's time we embraced such radical thinking. After all, democracy is not a destination, but a journey, one that thrives on continuous dialogue, evolution, and innovation. And a dash of the unexpected — like random selection — might just be the rejuvenating jolt our democracies need.

Political parties and representative democracy

So, what's the common denominator between the Norwegian bomber, the London rioters, and the Madrid sit-in? You may well ask. Each of these unsettling events hinged on one common theme — the seeming inability of elected officials to tune into the frequency of their demands. And how did they broadcast these grievances? Well, that would be the modern wonder that is new media.

The politicians and media never seem to escape the charge sheet when it comes to accusations of fanning the flames of extremism. The script seems to be set in stone — following such dramatic events, come the predictable calls for heavier regulation of political parties and the media. So, I say, let's scrutinize the case for tightening the reins on party regulation.

It's a universal truth — as solid as the recipe for a decent cup of tea — that representative democracy should be partnered with constitutional liberalism and an independent judicial system. These elements work to shield individuals and minorities from unwarranted government interference and majority oppression. Historically, this was considered sufficient, and political parties were generally allowed to roam free in their ideological playgrounds. But, has the playground morphed into a battlefield? Maybe, maybe not.

Mainstream parties seem to have misplaced their ideological DNA, leaving the clash of ideas to the David's of non-parliamentary smaller parties. Concurrently, there's been a rise in the musical-chairs style rotation within a two-party system. The result? Political parties have morphed into hazy coalitions of interests, propped up by large clandestine organizations nourished by an increasing supply of partisan jobs in government and regulated industries.

Now, it's easy to point fingers at the little guys. These smaller parties do manage to grab their fifteen minutes of fame, but often by adopting radical stances on single-issue policies – a strategy that can prove self-defeating. They're stuck in a rut, akin to the small suppliers dealing with large corporate entities. But perhaps, just as David defeated Goliath, these smaller parties could gain ground with stronger regulations on their larger counterparts.

Today, we can't ignore the wonders of the

digital age. The shift towards internet-based media could provide the slingshot the smaller parties need to challenge the big beasts. But just as our inboxes demanded protection from an influx of spam, the public may seek shelter from a barrage of minuscule parties.

So, while we might need to ramp up regulation, we have to do it with an artful finesse — one size doesn't fit all. Disclosure of membership should be a given for all parties, but the selection of electoral candidates, well that's a rulebook for the big boys. The same reasoning applies to their financing and access to broadcasting services.

An essential cog in the regulation machine is setting boundaries on campaign spending. Why? Because political campaigns have turned into marathons, and not the kind you can run with a foil blanket. This unfair race, monopolized by the incumbent leading parties, compromises effective public governance, and generates a "democracy fatigue".

Yet, despite the need to fine-tune the regulation of political parties, representation is still best served through broad political associations. Exploring other associations that focus on specific interests could lead us down a rabbit hole into a splintered society, teetering on the edge of anarchy or totalitarianism. So, let's aim to invigorate competition among parties, rather than search for new players in an already crowded game.

The anatomy of power inside political parties

Before we delve into the principles of representative democracy within political parties, let's first unpack the complex dynamics of power distribution that pulsate through their inner workings. This takes us down the path of organizational theory, as the power plays and struggles within political parties share some striking similarities with general organizational behavior.

Political parties have a distinct feature that makes them stand out - an insatiable hunger for power. This is perfectly summed up in the old saying, "In the other parties, I have adversaries; in my own party, I have enemies." Further, party organizations usually have members grouped together, creating an environment that feels somewhat tribal or feudal. This can result in two contrasting power-sharing scenarios. In some cases, the vanquished competitors are selectively invited to join the victors, while in others, they are shunned, leading to endless opposition or outright expulsion.

Groups form for myriad reasons, sometimes due to shared ideals or ideologies, but often the battles are over more mundane issues. A classic example is squabbling over an inconsequential amendment to the party's charter, which is promptly forgotten once the battle is won. Under communist regimes, power succession was often bizarrely determined by who got to plan the funeral of deceased leaders. In many parties, power is wielded by those who hold the keys to the courtroom, in the form of a courtier system.

In my short stint as a member of a Party Directorate, I identified three significant power sources within political parties: the Leader's inner circle, the Administration liaising with local party sections, and the Fundraisers.

The Leader's Cabinet usually consists of a small but influential group, including the head of the cabinet and secretary, media and intelligence liaison officers, and the head of administration. They orchestrate a network of official and unofficial political advisors whose roles vary considerably. Some are not members of the party or don't hold seats in the party's elected bodies. As policies change, so does the group's composition, but a select few maintain lasting influence over the leader. These power players are often behind the scenes and could include family members or party financiers.

Second in command is usually the Head of Administration, bearing titles like Secretary-General or Chief of Staff. His crucial role in overseeing party membership makes him integral to the leader's reelection. His power comes from his control over resources and his role in organizing party events and elections. However, the party's local organizational structure and selection process for national elections can sometimes undermine his influence.

Lastly, those responsible for fundraising play a critical role. This group can include a Party Treasurer, wealthy party donors, and dedicated fundraisers. While donors might sway policy direction, the dedicated fundraisers are the most active in peddling political favors and legislative votes to interest groups. Within this group, you'll often find some shady characters who are rewarded with sinecures or get a cut from the donations.

Understanding these dynamics is crucial before any regulation aimed at enhancing representative democracy within parties is considered. The discussion will need to address the relationships within local party sections, their role in candidate selection for national office, and the role of various national bodies representing the party.

Be aware of party youths

Think Portugal again. Could the tarnished reputations of José Sócrates and Miguel Relvas, along with the debatable dominance of the Party Youths ("Jotas") in Portugal's political landscape, be jeopardising the country's democratic future? Particularly when they fuel public scepticism over whether Portugal can claw its way out of its deep-seated social and moral crisis?

Is this grave threat enough grounds to trigger a state of emergency, stripping political leaders who are "Jotas" members of their political rights?

While emergencies can necessitate the temporary curtailment of some political rights to preserve democracy, these measures should be extreme rarities.

Over 2400 years ago, in the birthplace of democracy, this was the consensus. Athenians devised ostracism as a democratic safeguard. For a century, they held regular votes to banish for a decade anyone deemed a risk to democracy. This practice, starting in 506 BC and ending in 415 BC, was abused by organised groups that ousted political adversaries.

Fast forward to today, we've traded banishment for the suspension of political rights, primarily ineligibility for certain roles. The decision now rests with independent courts. These restrictions typically apply to organisations and individuals peddling constitutionally prohibited extremist ideologies - think neo-Nazi, neo-communist, racist, and xenophobic groups.

Yet, this system isn't immune to misuse, especially when states of emergency are declared, or non-independent courts call the shots. Look no further than the current scenarios in Venezuela and Russia for proof.

Therefore, unless we're dealing with terrorist groups, such suspensions should be a last resort. Indeed, that was the level-headed approach adopted in Portugal post-April 25th.

Must we, then, accept a bleak future sculpted by a mediocre "Jotas"-led political class? Not necessarily.

For starters, voters have the power to reject

"Jotas" candidates, provided their misgivings are laid bare to the public and the electorate comprehends their adverse implications. The easiest solution would be to require a minimum gardening leave of five years since leaving college. This would push political parties to scout for their candidates among competent professionals.

Simultaneously, university students can rise against the control of their academic associations by party-aligned youth. In achieving this, their party-neutral professors can enlighten them about the long-term effects of the "Jotas'" influence.

Ultimately, the most potent safeguard democracy has against its detractors is democracy itself, wielded through a candid and enlightened discussion on the role of partisan youth in democratic setups.

Direct election of party leaders: Pros and cons

The great pageant of democracy - casting our sacred votes in a free and fair election - should be the pride and joy of any political party. This grand ritual, the linchpin of a representative democracy, ought to be applied to our political parties themselves, wouldn't you agree?

After all, directly electing party leaders is a crowd-pleaser. It's as democratic as apple pie - giving every party member a megaphone and a say. Plus, it flings open the curtains on the party's internal bunfights, offering us mere voters a peep show into the minds and mantras of our prospective leaders.

But, as always, there's a but. Some overly enthusiastic cheerleaders of this principle are all for expanding it to all the party bigwigs, from national down to regional. On the other hand, there's a giddy faction that wants to fling open the doors and let anyone have a go, party member or not.

The former? Maybe they're on to something. Ensuring direct election might just need that. The latter? They're verging on lunacy. They seem to have mistaken political parties for some shiny new start-up, and election for a quirky product to flog to non-members. Parties aren't supposed to be relentless power-hungry machines seeking the fastest route to the throne.

However, before we all get misty-eyed over direct elections, let's peek at its underbelly. Remember the recent kerfuffle in the Portuguese Socialist Party? This system conveniently ignored the popular vote, hoisting up a leader nobody wanted, clinging on even in defeat. And let's not forget how it gives the home advantage to candidates backed by the party machinery, as evidenced by António José Seguro's not-so-surprising win.

Additionally, these direct elections suck the life out of subsequent debates, transforming the Congress into a dull coronation ceremony for the newly minted leader. So, before we jump headfirst into the shallow end of direct elections, let's keep our eyes wide open to its pitfalls and pratfalls.

Picture a gaggle of society folks, assembled in their fineries, not for some high-minded discourse, but to champion their pet interests. Replace the ballroom with political corridors and you have the political "baronies" - personal fiefdoms in a party devoid of ideology. For my Portuguese pals, the PSD springs to mind, doesn't it? With nary a whiff of a defined ideology, the party's folks are busy tending to their Barrosistas, Santanistas, or Cavaquistas, rather than identifying as liberals, social democrats, or Christian democrats.

Now, let's move on to a grand attempt to have the cake and eat it too - the mixed system of elections. Picture England, the land of the Big Ben and high teas, where electoral innovation knows no bounds. MPs, trade unionists, and youth organizations stroll into the electoral booth sporting different voter hats, casting different votes. A mash-up, if you will, between direct and indirect elections.

But the mixed system needs a dash of common sense – the elections for party bigwigs and for government office wannabes mustn't be lumped together like a bad shepherd's pie. In England, some party council leaders are barred from running for deputy or mayor. Only the national leadership can pop the question, and the council they'll represent gets to swipe right or left.

So, let's not be hasty with the roses and the thorns of direct elections. Let's simmer down, have a cup of Earl Grey, and sort out the tangled love triangle between party structures and the chosen gladiators for party or government positions. Only then, my dear, can we decide whether to embrace or to give the cold shoulder to the direct election method.

6 Electoral Systems and Representation

Electoral systems - those unheralded backstage hands of democracy's great play! They build the set where the thrilling drama of representation takes the spotlight. Come, join me on this intellectual romp as we grapple with the question of the 'just-right' MP headcount, the enigma of professional politicians, the lure of nominal constituencies, the finesse in defining constituencies, and the intriguing concept of weighted electoral systems.

First up, let's imagine we're Goldilocks at the MP-count buffet. How many helpings do we need for a hearty democratic meal? Too skimpy a serving, and we're left with an unfulfilled electorate. Too lavish, and we're stewing in bureaucratic bloat and complexity. It's less a stab in the dark, more a deliberate dish best served with diverse voices and manageable governance.

Now, let's turn to the curious case of professional politicians. Are they the Oracle at Delphi, brimming with political wisdom, or just crafty foxes raiding the public henhouse? Push cynicism aside, these career politicos do inject a level of know-how and steadiness into the mix. But let's not forget the risk of them floating in their political bubble, disconnected from the reality of the ordinary Joes and Janes. It's all about teetering on the tightrope between knowledge and ground-level representation.

Onwards to the cosy nooks of nominal constituencies. Picture this - one specific geographical area cosying up to one representative. The common folks have a name, a face, a human peg to hang their political hat on. But like any love story, there are thorny bits - gerrymandering, where the art of drawing boundaries veers into the dark alley of political manipulation.

Then there's the artful task of defining constituencies, as delicate as slicing a Victoria sponge at a British high tea. The pieces need to be balanced, taking into account population, socio-economic factors, and geographic continuity. It's not just a matter of counting heads, but a high stakes balancing act between diversity and fair representation.

Finally, let's tiptoe into the sleek halls of weighted electoral systems. Think of it as an electoral scale, balancing constituencies of different sizes and populations. It aims to give every vote an equal twirl on the democratic dance floor, irrespective of the voter's postcode. A charming notion, but the critics have a point - it can skew representation and muddy the democratic waters.

So, there you have it - a rollicking roller-coaster ride through the theme park of electoral systems and representation. Like any robust democracy, it's a never-ending debate, a ceaseless balancing act, and a constantly evolving work of political art.

Representation versus representativeness

Representation versus representativeness—sounds like a semantic squabble, doesn't it? But, like night and day, they're vastly different. Representation is the ubiquitous wallflower, happily existing in any political system, democratic or otherwise. Representativeness, however, is the life of the democratic party—freely elected representatives presiding over a government, buoyed by individual and universal suffrage. The study of voting theory delves into the labyrinth of how voters can select representatives that truly mirror their will. The subject covers an array of voting systems for the selection of candidates, summarised neatly on this Wikipedia page (https://en.wikipedia.org/wiki/Electoral_system).

In the realm of Portuguese legislation, candidates are cherry-picked from a single closed party list, using the proportional Hondt method. Therefore, to effectively assess the system for electing Deputies to the Assembly of the Republic, we need to dissect both the method of proportionality and the list system.

When it comes to proportionality, we should

separately scrutinise full proportionality, semi-proportionality, and block voting systems, before delving into the nitty-gritty techniques applicable to each. In Portugal, the full proportionality system was the chosen one, but after a solid 35 years, one can't help but wonder about the benefits of swapping it out for a semi-proportional system.

One such variant, the so-called cumulative vote within a two-round voting system, has potential to eliminate the prevalent underrepresentation of deputies, and dispel parties' temptation to put forward yes-man lists curated by the party directory. For instance, in the case of Castelo Branco constituency parties could offer their roster of eight candidates for the four up-for-grabs seats, with voters having ten votes to distribute among their party's candidates. Here, the candidates' pecking order on the list would lose its relevance, breaking the parties' stranglehold on who makes it to the second round. Furthermore, we can envisage a system in which, in the second round, voters can divvy up their votes among candidates from different parties. This is but one illustration of the numerous systems we can engineer to curb, without eliminating, the influence of party directories in the electoral process.

Before we pull out the paintbrushes and

dabble with political reform, let's make one thing clear. Boosting the calibre of Portuguese politicians isn't about throwing a handful of new policies into the mix, hoping for the best. It involves a harmonious blend of electing an optimal number of deputies and rolling out an electoral system that rings true with the ethos of representative democracy.

To drive my point home, let me paint you a picture—rather a bit simplified, admittedly. Imagine bidding goodbye to the current system where a select few—half a dozen, excluding municipalities—wield the power to pick the occupants of over 5,000 political seats. Instead, picture a streamlined version where around 300 elected officials have the reins, choosing and overseeing the holders of a more manageable 2,000 political seats in the State and Public Companies. I'm not peddling a panacea here, but it's certainly a step towards a more transparent, more representative democracy.

"MPs - too many, too few, or too inept?"

There's this common gripe in Portugal: a dissatisfaction with the subpar quality of the Assembly of the Republic's deputies. The solutions touted lash the number of deputies or fatten their paychecks to lure in those with more to offer. Yet the reality, my friends, is that these tried-and-tested strategies have done nothing but wreak havoc on the core principles of representative democracy.

To grasp the futility of these efforts, all you need to do is glance back at Portugal's own political track record. When the first legislature of the 3rd Republic kicked off in 1976, there were 263 deputies at the ready. By 1979, they had culled this herd to 250, and in 1991, further whittled it down to the current tally of 230.

So, what's the golden number? To strike a balance between proportionality and effectiveness, we need to dig a little deeper. This takes us beyond the numbers game and right into the foundations of our constitution, our electoral system, and the nature of our political regimes.

This isn't a task for the faint-hearted. It demands an informed, robust debate about the deputies' role and the various strategies that would gel with a representative regime. Just to give you a taster, consider these four hot-button issues: the election (or not) of executive members, carving out electoral districts, the part direct democracy plays, and the professionalization of political roles.

So, before we go on a deputy-diet or decide to throw more money at the problem, let's remember - democracy isn't a business. Let's tackle this issue with the seriousness it deserves.

Pouring More into the Deputy Pot: Quantity, Quality, and Cutbacks? Direct democracy, it's a bit of a gamble, isn't it? I find myself squarely in the camp of those favouring accountable politicians, predominantly those unmarred by professional politics, yet glowing with a sense of public service. And here's the kicker - I'm an advocate for a meaty upswing in the number of deputies, twinned with a robust cut in their pay.

Run some simple arithmetic on Portugal's 9 million voters. Let's say a single deputy can effectively represent 15,000 to 30,000 voters. The outcome? We'd need somewhere between 300 and 600 deputies. An intermediate number, you might argue, would be more appropriate. But let's leave that quibble to a detailed study. For now, let's contrast this with the 42,000 voters currently sharing the attention of each deputy.

Next stop, our European neighbours. Countries of a similar size to Portugal. We're rubbing shoulders with the Czech Republic and Belgium in the league of the lowest numbers of deputies. Languishing below the average of high-deputy countries like Hungary, Sweden, and Greece.

Oh, and let's not forget our comparisons closer to home. The professionals who keep our country ticking over: 273 people per doctor, 384 per lawyer, 1,761 per dentist, and 6,211 per judicial magistrate. And let's not leave out the private sector - BCP with 14,400 shareholders per non-executive director, BPI with 1,100.

Any way you slice it, there's a gaping hole where there should be Portuguese deputies, not an excess. That's why, in the face of an online petition clamouring for a reduction in MPs, we've rallied our own call-to-arms: an increase in deputies.

However, let's not put the cart before the horse. We can't pin down the ideal number of deputies without a calm, enlightened discussion about their professional status and the representation model we want for Portugal –

topics I'll be sinking my teeth into in my upcoming pieces.

MPs Pay: Duty or a slice of professionalism?

The question of deputy dosh has a knack for splitting the Portuguese populace neatly into two rival camps. One team, let's call them the 'populists', bemoan that deputies are paid handsomely for their limited qualifications and contributions. The other side, our 'technocrats', argue we should loosen the purse strings even more to lure higher calibre folk into Parliament. Unfortunately, both sides miss the mark if they bypass what a deputy's role should be - executive or non-executive? Let's run our eyes over the facts.

Post the 25th of April, the deputy's salary has held steady at half of the President's. Roll back to 2008, a deputy's wage clocked in at about nine times the minimum wage. In the grand scheme of salaries - particularly when eyeballing senior roles in companies and state roles - it's a modest pay package for deputies with similar training. What's more, over time, it's become more of a relative pittance. The President's salary, which in 1984 was 25.6 times the minimum wage, had shrunk to a mere 17.4 times by 2008.

However, this salary story takes a sharp turn when we consider deputies' add-on earnings. Their retirement pensions, for one, are served up well before the ripe age of 65. At one point, a deputy elected at 18 could be lounging in a pension-funded life of luxury at 26! Today, even after several recalibrations, it's an offensively generous pot. Not to mention the allowances and grants that have swollen from modest portions in 1984 to account for over 50% of a deputy's base salary today.

While we can squabble over whether these sums are fair or not, the key reminder is that remuneration for political roles can be approached from two starkly contrasting angles: do we uphold the principle of public service or pivot towards the principle of professionalisation?

Public Service or Professional Politics: A Paradox for the Ages. In the past, the principle of public service was king. The belief was that public service was a kind of noble volunteer work, deserving of only expense reimbursement and a symbolic stipend. Nowadays, non-exec roles, like those undertaken by deputies, are becoming full-time gigs, often pursued exclusively. If this trend tickles our fancy, their pay should align with public servants, and factor in their qualifications and level of responsibility.

Both models - public service and professional politics - have a place in our theoretical framework, so long as they align with our representative democracy. But, to pick a side, we need to weigh up which better upholds the principle of representativeness. And this needs a careful balancing act: looking at electoral districts, their geographical spread, their proportionality in voter representation, and the definition of political roles (in State and Autonomous Bodies) to be filled by elected representatives.

Let's chew on this: should government members also be deputies? Our constitution doesn't demand it, and the outcome has been a two-tier failure — poor quality leaders and a Parliament lacking representation.

The case in point is the Prime Minister, who needn't be an elected deputy and has carte blanche to recruit their cabinet and "boys" as they see fit. With such a system, the quality of leaders in the thousands of unelected political roles oscillates between enlightened despotism and blundering obscurity at the whim of the PM. A snapshot of the present-day spectacle reveals a cast of junior ministers, often fresh-faced interns from youth political groups or lobby-fodder from sector interests.

Finally, any discussion about the pros and cons of professionalising non-exec political roles must tie into the debate around the independence we must grant public servants. And, in particular, their selection, promotion, and powers.

To paint a picture of the significance of these choices, contrast the typical municipal management models pre- and post-25th of April. Earlier, the model was a mayor dropping by the Town Hall for an hour or two at the end of the day for a chat with the Chief Secretary. Nowadays, any small municipality employs a full-time Mayor, several councillors, advisers, and parish presidents. The result? Inevitably, they end up treading on the toes of senior and middle management.

Democratic Institutions: Pay Less, Get More? The cost of democracy shouldn't have us clutching our wallets in horror. That's why our preference leans towards a salary structure rooted in the ideals of public service. In line with this, we're suggesting a rather symbolic base salary for deputies. Say, something along the lines of 30% of the President's salary — sounds reasonable, doesn't it? This change in pay could let us bolster the number of deputies to 300, while simultaneously trimming the overall budget of the Assembly of the Republic (party grants and election campaigns aside) by about 5%. A lower price tag for a higher headcount — quite the democratic deal, wouldn't you say?

Vote for parties or MPs?

If there ever was a gulf more unbridgeable than that of political parties and their voters, we're witnessing it now, in all its splendid isolation. It's like those eerie secret societies we read about in novels, except these are the real deal, clandestine corridors of power adorned with vested interests.

Moreover, there's a mirror problem of sorts. Our dear voters, bless their hearts, don't really see their own reflections in the parliamentarians they've put in place. How can they when they can't even keep track of the players' names? I mean, do you know who your representative is? Because, I'll admit it – I haven't the foggiest!

Some casual browsing on the Assembly of the Republic website shed some, rather harsh, light on this disconnection. Take my constituency for example – the one that voted our esteemed Prime Minister José Socrates into power, Castelo Branco. Despite being represented by a meagre four deputies, not one of them was directly elected. Talk about absentee landlords! In a single year, a grand total of eleven deputies took a turn at these four seats. I felt like I was watching a game of musical chairs!

So, we're compelled to ask: are these folks genuinely representative? The principle of representativeness is more than just a numbers game, more than proportional ticks against votes and mandates, or deputies and voters. It's about inclusivity, the buzzword of the decade.

The criticisms that our parliament is lacking in diversity, that it's not truly reflective of the heterogeneous fabric of our society, are not entirely without basis. Be it gender, profession, religion, or any other individual trait (wealth, education, age, or race, pick your choice), or even collective identifiers (tribe, social class, club, etc.), the representation seems to be skewed.

And while we're on this train of thought, let's not forget the so-called 'legitimacy' of group representation. A few active lobbies have managed to sneak their soldiers into the battlefield, inflating their ranks. Portugal's law on electoral lists, for example, was seemingly put to good use to bolster the number of women in parliament. I'd call that clever, if not for the fact that it's further muddying the waters of representativeness.

However, let's not forget that the rallying cries of specific groups, no matter how socially palatable, should never bulldoze over individual rights, at the risk of trampling on the cardinal rules of representativeness and equality within a system of individual and universal suffrage.

It makes me ponder: isn't the very edifice of representative democracy tottering precariously on the brink? Lately, we're hearing more calls for a more direct form of democracy—referendums, petitions, you name it. Yet, history has given us ample warnings about the perils of direct democracy. It's like a lollipop given to a child: sweet at first but rotten in the long run, as it's readily exploited by smooth-talking demagogues and often ends up spiralling into dictatorship.

Still, we can't bury our heads in the sand and ignore that the leaps and bounds made in information technology have now made it possible for voters to champion their own cause without the fuss or the need for middlemen.

In reality, any legitimate clampdown on the rule of individual representativeness should only be borne out of efficacy. It's not rocket science to see that a parliament of a mere half-dozen deputies hardly carry the stamp of representativeness. By the same token, a parliament filled to the brim with thousands of deputies is much like a toothless tiger—unable to get anything done, thereby losing its representativeness. And for those of you who require an example, we only need to cast a glance at the alleged people's democracies of communist nations.

Equally, the selection of one or several candidates, in one or multiple rounds, using more or less proportional methods, does not provide a free pass to delegate a right that is, by definition, individual to groups. This principle of non-transferability of this individual right holds true even for political parties, irrespective of whether we regard them as associations of voters with shared ideas or merely another interest group.

So, to wrap this up, ensuring the representativeness of elected deputies is no mean feat—it's not simply about making it easier for independent candidates to come forward, or implementing open list systems. The bedrock principle that legitimises those elected is rooted in their immovability, and that they can only be supplanted by a fresh election, not by alternates handpicked by party bigwigs.

So, to vote for parties or deputies? Now, that's a question we'd do well to ponder over.

What kind of constituencies?

Teetering on the tightrope of representativeness involves a heated discourse on the electoral system. Two fiery subjects often make the headlines—its geographical delineation (be it administratively, regionally, or population-based) and the nature of voting systems (think proportional or mixed systems, and the conundrum of closed versus open lists).

True representativeness calls for closeness, a sense of familiarity. However, this requirement of proximity becomes a chameleon, changing hues depending on the purpose of representation—local or universal causes. So, deciding on an acceptable number of deputies is not just about counting heads, but also hinges on the arrangement of electoral districts and lists.

To illustrate, let's assume that a deputy should represent no fewer than 15,000 voters but no more than 30,000. In Portugal, where lists comprise multiple candidates—let's say a minimum of five—the constituency would need to cater to between 75,000 and 150,000 voters. Now, compare this with England where a single-candidate system holds sway. Here, each constituency would house between 15,000 and 30,000 voters. The upshot, in terms of converting votes into mandates, would be strikingly different, despite the universality of the voting right in both countries.

Now, let's consider Portugal again. One of the signatories of the current online petition demanding a trim down of MPs says, "We want professional MPs who represent their regions". Taking this at face value, we'd need a paltry three deputies, given the three regions—Mainland, Azores, and Madeira. If we factor in districts, we'd end up with 18 deputies. But wait, if we consider municipalities, the tally shoots up to 308 deputies—way above the 180 that our petitioner has in mind. And should we decide to throw Parish Councils into the mix, we'd be drowning in an ocean of 4,240 deputies—a number so far-fetched it borders on the ludicrous.

Nevertheless, the proposal of choosing a lone representative for each administrative unit in Portugal smacks of absurdity. Let's take municipalities as an example. If the system was applied, the tiny electorate of 337 in Corvo municipality in the Azores would elect a single deputy. Meanwhile, the bustling metropolis of Lisbon, teeming with 513,931 voters, would also elect just one deputy. Now, if that's not a slap in the face of representativeness, I don't know what is.

The choice of other alternative geographic

units, namely parishes, comarcas or NUTs III is also not a solution for defining the desirable number of deputies. This is because degrees of proportionality below one hundred (with or without the Hondt method) have to be justified by transparent criteria such as the degree of geographic dispersion, transport accessibility or the number of legislative chambers foreseen in the constitutional system.

In conclusion, constituencies should be defined based on representativeness and not administrative criteria. However, its definition must take into account not only the total number of deputies but also the desired voting system.

Simple vs. weighted voting systems

Representation and representativeness, though similar, are not the same. While representation can be found in any political system, including non-democratic ones, representativeness is exclusively tied to democracies, where governance is achieved by representatives elected through individual and universal suffrage. Voting theory delves into how voters can elect representatives that are genuinely representative of their desires and perspectives. Today, this theory explores various voting systems for choosing one or more candidates, succinctly outlined on this Wikipedia page (https://en.wikipedia.org/wiki/Electoral_system).

In Portugal's legislative process, multiple candidates are selected from a single, closed party list using the proportional Hondt method. Therefore, in order to accurately evaluate the system for electing Deputies to the Assembly of the Republic, it's necessary to separately assess the proportionality method and the list system.

In terms of proportionality, it's crucial to independently examine the systems of absolute proportionality, semi-proportionality, and block voting before separately analyzing the techniques we can employ for each. Although Portugal has opted for a system of absolute proportionality, after more than three and a half decades, it's worth questioning the benefits of transitioning to a semi-proportional system.

One variant, the so-called cumulative voting in a two-round system, could significantly address the representation deficit of current deputies and discourage parties from submitting lists of "yes-men" from the party directory. For instance, in the Castelo Branco constituency that we referred to before, parties could present their list of 8 candidates for the 4 available seats. However, voters would have 10 votes to distribute among the candidates of their choice, rendering the candidate order on the list irrelevant. This system would also disrupt the parties' monopoly on who advances to the second round. Moreover, it's feasible to conceive a system where, in the second round, voters can allocate their votes to candidates across different parties. This is just one example of the various systems we can design to curb, though not eliminate, the role of party directories in the electoral process.

Notwithstanding the need for other ancillary legislation to reform political parties and their funding laws, we underline that elevating the calibre of Portuguese politicians requires the concurrent selection of an appropriate number of deputies and an electoral system that encourages the establishment of a truly representative democracy.

Voting systems: majority vs plurality

Democracy, in its many forms, adopts diverse electoral systems to determine its representatives. Two of the most common are Majority and Plurality Voting Systems. Both have merits and demerits which can significantly influence the political landscape, shaping the prevalence of bi-partisan outcomes or multi-party alliances.

Majority Voting Systems, often embodied in run-off elections or instant-runoff voting, demand that a candidate secure more than half of the total votes to be declared the winner. This system has a tendency to encourage moderation, as candidates strive for a broad appeal to clinch over 50% of the votes. Furthermore, it upholds a degree of political stability by avoiding power fragmentation, which can lead to legislative deadlock.

However, a notable disadvantage of Majority Voting Systems is the risk of voter attrition in successive rounds of voting, as citizens may become disenfranchised with the process or face hurdles in multiple trips to the polls. Additionally, these systems may disadvantage smaller parties and independent candidates who struggle to achieve broad appeal, thereby fostering a two-party system.

An illustrative example of a Majority Voting System is France's presidential election. The system promotes a two-round runoff which, despite occasionally leading to an "election by default" in the second round, ensures the elected president has the support of the majority of voters.

Plurality Voting Systems, or first-past-the-post systems, declare the candidate with the most votes in their constituency the winner, regardless of whether they have achieved an absolute majority. This system, common in the UK and the US, simplifies the electoral process and facilitates clear-cut results.

However, the Plurality Voting System's primary drawback is its potential to overlook the diversity of voter preferences. A candidate may be elected with less than 50% of the vote, meaning the majority of voters preferred other candidates. Furthermore, it may encourage tactical voting, where voters support the "least bad" option among the likely winners, rather than their preferred candidate. The system is also criticized for promoting a two-party system, to the detriment of minor parties and independents.

The implementation of a minimum threshold in Plurality Voting Systems can mitigate these effects. A minimum threshold compels parties to obtain a certain percentage of votes to be eligible for representation. This mechanism aims to balance the desire for broad representation with the need for governmental stability.

However, while this may foster multi-party representation, it could potentially exclude smaller parties, paradoxically reducing the diversity of political voices. An example of this is Turkey, where a high threshold of 10% has often resulted in many votes being effectively discarded, and power being concentrated in fewer parties.

The choice between Majority and Plurality Voting Systems significantly influences whether a political system leans towards bipartisan or multi-party outcomes. Majority Voting Systems can lead to a concentration of power, typically resulting in a two-party system. This scenario is evident in the US, where Democrats and Republicans dominate. Conversely, Plurality Voting Systems, especially those with a reasonable minimum threshold, may encourage a more diverse, multi-party system, such as in the Netherlands.

In conclusion, both Majority and Plurality Voting Systems carry their unique set of advantages and disadvantages. Their influence on the political landscape, in terms of promoting bipartisan or multi-party outcomes, is profound. Therefore, choosing an appropriate voting system is vital to the representation and stability of a democracy. The goal should be to optimize the electoral process to reflect the will of the electorate while maintaining a functional and stable political environment.

7 Democracy and Equality

This chapter dives headfirst into the sprawling, often confusing, tangle that is the relationship between democracy and equality. These two old pals, touted as cornerstones of our modern societies, can sometimes behave more like bickering siblings. Sure, democracy, with its star-spangled promise of being a governance "of the people, by the people, and for the people," sounds like a beacon of equality. But when we shine a light on the harsh disparities of wealth distribution, we're left squirming in our seats, pondering how this noble ideal actually measures up.

Our opening act, "Political Contributions and Democracy," strips bare the cozy relationship between money bags and political clout. We peek under the covers at how heavy-duty donations can manipulate policy and steer governance, crowning a privileged few as 'elite' citizens who swing a bigger bat in the democratic game.

Next up, "Democracy and Wealth Inequality" takes us on a riveting tour of the economic terrain of today's democracies. As we traverse the growing chasms between the haves and have-nots, we'll grapple with how these deepening fault lines shake the foundations of our democratic ethos and weaken our social weave.

"Money Talks," our third stop, trains its lens on the commanding voice of wealth in democracies. It seems cash doesn't just purchase the latest gadgets or gourmet meals; it has an unnerving knack for bending public opinion, tipping electoral scales, and even scribbling laws. This unsettling truth compels us to question our democratic health check and brainstorm how we can tune it up to sing a more harmonious tune.

Well, we've come a long way from the fear that democracy would let the poor play Robin Hood, seizing the riches of the wealthy. If we look at Uncle Sam's backyard, we might even say we're witnessing the reverse. Cracking this enigma is the purpose of "Sugar-Coating the Poor".

"Can't Afford Democracy" — a title that stings with irony — delves into the escalating price tag of democratic participation. Be it the dizzying heights of campaign costs or the eye-watering expenses for quality education, healthcare, or legal aid, we chew over how these financial hurdles could thwart the democratic vow of equal participation.

To wrap up, "Democracy and Meritocracy" wrestles with the spiky question of merit versus equality in a democratic ring. Meritocracy, with its glossy promise of an unbiased battle where only grit and talent score points, seems fair game. But with the scoreboard tilted by glaring inequalities, one has to ask: how level is this playing field, really?

Finally, in "Multiculturalism and Democracy," we spice things up by throwing culture into the mix, and let me tell you, it's like a thrilling dance of representation across borders and traditions.

This chapter offers a robust and jargon-free dissection of democracy's tangled relationship with equality. Be prepared for a no-holds-barred journey through some uncomfortable truths and tantalizing possibilities. So, sit back, buckle up, and let's get this democratic dialogue started.

Political contributions and democracy

Democracy, like most things in life, has become a rather pricey affair. To get a sense of the astronomical costs involved, cast your mind back to 2008 when American presidential candidates managed to raise a head-spinning $1.8 billion in campaign funds, a whopping 80% leap from 2004. Barack Obama, the Democratic candidate, alone pulled in a staggering $745.7 million in private funds. Who knew winning hearts and minds came with such a hefty price tag?

In a precedent-shattering move, Obama snubbed public funds for his general election campaign, the first time a major party nominee had ever done so. Now, that's a twist in the tale! But does this shake-up merit applause or concern? And what, pray tell, does this say about the state of our representative democracy?

The debate between public and private financing isn't new, and it's a bit of a sticky wicket. Particularly prickly is how private financing can lend an unfair leg-up to incumbents and special interest groups like trade unions and business associations, tipping the democratic scales in their favour.

In an ideal world, the principle of free association would skip merrily hand-in-hand with the principle of free financing. But here's the rub: when public office comes with the perk of decisions that can line private pockets, the scales get skewed. The tempting lure of financial gain can overshadow the altruistic call of public service, making the principle of free financing a pipe dream in representative systems.

Under representative democracy, the proposed remedy is to slap a cap on campaign spending and limit its source to public funds. This approach aims to level the playing field and keep democracy's game fair.

But let's turn our gaze to nations cozied up to representative democracy. Shouldn't candidates have the freedom to strike deals with special interest groups? Picture this: Party A could promise to ease financial regulations, boost private outsourcing of public services, or increase arms spending, all in return for generous campaign contributions.

However, this trade-off is easier said than done. Why, you ask? Well, creating a competitive marketplace for political funding is a non-starter, thanks to the uneven nature of benefits received by special interest groups and the general public. For instance, if deregulation could net one thousand banks a tidy $100 million each, while 200 million voters could save $1,000 each through enhanced deposit protection, the banks have a clear advantage. The voters' potential savings don't stand a chance against the bankers' definite gains.

So, it's clear as day that representative democracy needs a firm hand on the tiller when it comes to regulating political contributions. Every democratic nation enforces some form of regulation, such as limiting donations from foreign entities, public service contractors, trade unions, and regulated corporations. These are typically accompanied by rules on public disclosure.

However, let's not be naive. These regulations can be sidestepped using a variety of back doors: foundations, think tanks, media outlets, and other unrelated intermediaries. Therefore, to keep the democratic race fair, we need to tighten our grip. This means clamping down on the size of donations, limiting advertising, and so on. But remember, these constraints need to be rooted in the principles of constitutional liberalism. Otherwise, we risk losing the dynamic interplay between market capitalism, constitutional liberalism, and representative democracy, a powerful trio that forms the lifeblood of our society.

Wealth inequality and democracy

Democracy and wealth inequality are like dancers in a complex ballet; their steps are entwined in intricate patterns that confuse as much as they enlighten. The World Bank suggests that capitalist nations tend to have less poverty and inequality than their non-capitalist counterparts. Yet, a look at the OECD lineup brings the situation into stark relief - wealth inequality varies dramatically. Chile and Denmark are two striking examples. Chile, the highest scorer on the inequality league table, manages to make Denmark, the most equal, look like a model of harmony.

The granddames of democracy - the USA, UK, and Israel - don't quite score top marks on equality either. This curious detail begs the question - is democracy a silent accomplice or a white knight in the battle against wealth inequality?

We must resist the temptation to oversimplify and draw hasty conclusions. Staunch democratic countries often become irresistible magnets for the super-rich. But let's be clear, these democracies are not necessarily mass-producing billionaires. They're more like well-decorated shops with an open-door policy for the world's wealthiest.

A fascinating way to dissect this puzzling relationship is to compare the wealth and happiness league tables with democracy scorecards. For example, the Economist Democracy Index for 2022 pitches Denmark in 6th place while Chile comes in at 19th, neck and neck with the UK. Israel and the US, interestingly, are demoted to the 'flawed democracy' category, ranking 29th and 30th. The World Happiness Report for 2023 only adds another layer of complexity. Denmark ranks second, while the US, UK, Israel, and Chile paint a kaleidoscope of happiness rankings.

The causality conundrum, however, remains stubbornly intact. The relationship between democracy and wealth inequality is a maze. Democracy might influence wealth through its policies, either levelling the playing field or creating an environment fertile for wealth creation. But the true impact of democratic governance on wealth distribution is often clouded by the global flow of wealth to these democratic havens.

The key to unlock this puzzle? A formidable task - dissecting wealth both before and after public transfers. A task that, as of September 2021, remains undone. This emphasizes the tangled web that this issue weaves and the crying need for in-depth research to untangle it.

In summary, it's crucial to approach this topic with an open mind and not hastily jump to conclusions. The relationship between democracy and wealth inequality is a winding path, strewn with hidden twists and turns. Understanding it demands more than surface-level scrutiny. It calls for a deep dive into how democratic processes and wealth distribution affect each other, an expedition that's as daunting as it's fascinating.

Money talks

The Democratic Paradox: When money speaks louder than words. In the grand drama of modern capitalism, business tycoons often play the villains, cast as cold-hearted money-machines. Yet, offstage, many of them don a different mask - the generous philanthropist, championing democratic causes. They can be relentless in their quest for profit, but when it comes to giving it away, their wallets fling open. The riddle that arises from this duality begs for answers. Are they driven by self-interest, guilt, vanity, or perhaps institutional obligation? To untangle this knot, let's take a tour across the United States, where philanthropy has deep roots.

In the financial year of 2014, Americans, displaying their generous spirits, donated an impressive $358.38 billion, a jump of 7.1% from the preceding year. Corporate coffers poured in $17.77 billion, marking a sizeable 13.7% uptick from 2013. These philanthropic downpours represented 2.1% of the GDP, with half targeted at religious and educational ventures. To give some perspective, this philanthropic spending outstripped the $148.18 billion that the US government contributed as international net official development assistance in 2013.

What does this tell us? Well, the private sector can become a gushing fount of funds for redistribution, given the right environment. A vibrant testament to this are foundations such as The Carter Center, Protect Democracy, World Learning, Eurasia Foundation, Freedom House, Unlock Democracy, Defending Rights and Dissent, Involve Foundation, and Patchwork Foundation, each striving to fortify democracy domestically and overseas.

Still, even these foundations are not immune to criticism. Accusations vary, from disregarding the founders' mandates to overzealously propagating their ideologies. George Soros's Open Society, for instance, is a regular target of critics, despite its notable efforts to foster democratic policies in hostile environments, including Soros's own homeland, Hungary.

Interestingly, when it comes to the impact on democracy, personal philanthropy vastly outshines corporate donations. The former, generally given freely and transparently, contrasts sharply with the latter, which often come with terms and conditions and a lack of transparency. The sheer volume of corporate funds can, at times, tilt the scales of democracy.

Therefore, it is important to draw a clear line between personal and corporate philanthropy. The former, driven by individual conviction, aims for the common good without expecting immediate returns. In contrast, corporate philanthropy, often tethered to PR or strategic interests, can veer dangerously close to manipulating democratic processes.

In the final analysis, the enigma of capitalists as philanthropists may have diverse explanations, but the positive impact of their generosity is irrefutable. Their contributions are invaluable to many democratic causes. Yet, the narrative needs to shift towards promoting transparent and unconditional giving, especially within the corporate world. For when money talks, it should echo the spirit of democracy, equality, and shared prosperity. Despite its pitfalls, philanthropy, if pursued with honesty and transparency, can serve as a formidable bulwark of democracy.

Sugar-coating the poor

Well, we've come a long way from the fear that democracy would let the poor play Robin Hood, seizing the riches of the wealthy. If we look at Uncle Sam's backyard, we might even say we're witnessing the reverse.

Cracking this enigma is like trying to decode the grandest riddle of American politics. Christopher Jencks tries his hand at the puzzle in Our Unequal Democracy. And yet, he overlooks a pair of crucial elements – the pesky diminishing returns in taxation and the cunning "sugar-coating of the poorer among the poor".

The former's a tale as old as time: the rich can splash their cash on top-notch tax planning, and when the taxman turns up, they squirrel their fortunes away, faster than a rabbit in a fox's den.

The latter is often shrugged off as a melodrama exclusive to the economies less touched by fortune. Imagine Chavez and his populist cronies, buttering up their power base by doling out a slice of income among the neediest to secure their popularity. It's a technique even criminals swear by when they concoct their own little welfare system in the back alleys they lord over.

But what we fail to acknowledge is that the American tableau, where the bottom half of the populace barely faces any income tax, is akin to the same strategy. Only, this policy's bill has been footed by the remaining 45% of the not-so-rich lot, primarily the middle and upper-middle strata.

This brings us to a pair of deliciously intriguing questions we'll revisit down the line. First, why did representative democracy safeguard the wealthy yet flunked at devising a more equitable tax system focused on expenditure and wealth over income? Second, are those at the bottom rung actually reaping benefits from these income tax exemptions? Now, there's some food for thought.

Can't afford democracy?

Democracy and freedom are entwined like a Gordian knot - one does not exist without the other. Individual liberty, free from hurdles and constraints, and collective liberty, the ability to take the reins of one's life, both underscore freedom's inherent flexibility. However, the menu of options that democracy lays out is not equally palatable to all. For those at the economic fringes, the practicality of a hot meal may outweigh lofty democratic ideals. While this might make the rest of us balk, it pinpoints a sobering truth: freedom comes with a price tag.

Capitalism, with its predilection for wealth creation, is a high-stakes game where the payoff can be a lush landscape of choices. This system doesn't just elevate your bank balance; it extends its golden touch to fundamental freedoms often overlooked in the balance sheets.

Think about it. Capitalists' thirst to hawk their products stimulates freedom of thought, belief, opinion, and expression. Their need to access diverse channels for consumer outreach necessitates a free media. It's like a domino effect. And then there's the freedom of information, a prerequisite for savvy commercial and investment choices. Market capitalism hates asymmetrical information as much as a cat hates water, because it messes with the efficiency of markets.

Freedom of association is another gem in the democratic-capitalist crown. It's a linchpin of democracy, vital for representation, and a star player in capitalism, enabling the pooling of private property into collective ownership. Capitalism also cleverly curtails risk by separating personal and corporate responsibility through limited liability - a masterstroke for nurturing entrepreneurial dreams.

Nevertheless, these freedoms aren't an open invitation for corporations to turn democracy into their personal playground. Freedom of expression isn't a license to pull the wool over consumers' and investors' eyes. Freedom of assembly isn't a permit for shady, anti-competitive manoeuvres. Rights have their boundaries - they aren't carte blanche to establish cartels or engage in insider trading.

Setting these boundaries is a tightrope walk. It necessitates an intricate understanding of democracy - both its representative form and its distorted doppelgängers. Only the former has a valid pass for the pursuit of liberty.

In wrapping up, let's not be too hasty to brand people as either simpletons or Machiavellian schemers. Freedom's constraints need thoughtful examination and, if there's any doubt, we should err on the side of liberty. By acknowledging the economic keys that unlock freedom, we can pave the way for an inclusive democracy where freedom isn't the exclusive domain of the well-off, but a universal birthright.

Democracy and meritocracy

Market capitalism is commonly bellowed as the epitome of meritocracy - a nifty little system where those blessed with talent and hard graft get the juiciest bits of the pie. So, what's the score with democracy? Do we see the same principles in play? Well, let's pop on our specs and have a look-see.

If we're handing out medals for meritocracy, Canada, Norway, Finland, and Denmark are doing a splendid job. They've got a lid on inherited income advantages, ensuring that Daddy Warbucks can only hand down less than a fifth of his wealth. But across the pond, in the US, UK, and Italy, it's a rather different story - social mobility appears to be chained to parental education levels, a rather sobering thought.

Another quirk of capitalism is its occasional bout of fumbleitis when dealing with long-term human capital investment. Just picture those bright-eyed graduates, bursting with knowledge, skill, and debt, being shunted into low-skill jobs. This cringe-inducing disconnect could be due to cyclic market trends or specific market glitches, but let's not kid ourselves - it's not capitalism's finest hour.

And let's not forget those industries where

hopeful jobseekers pile up like cars in a traffic jam, especially those snazzy 'winner-takes-all' sectors. The entertainment industry springs to mind, with its alluring allure of superstardom luring in legions of aspirants. Yet for most, the glitter fades to a humdrum existence of slinging drinks or flipping burgers, their expensive art school credentials gathering dust.

Let's also tip our hats to the impact of cyclical shifts, with the teaching profession being a prime example. The demand for teachers dances to the tune of population growth and policy changes. The 1950s baby boom, followed by the 1960s economic boom, led to a swell in school enrollments. Yet, when fertility rates dipped, the pendulum swung the other way, hurling teachers from their pedestal of respect into the bleak landscape of unemployment or low-wage work.

Educational returns hinge on a myriad of factors, not least of which is parenting, but the invisible hand of supply and demand looms large over income and status. It's the flexibility demanded by the marketplace, but this flexibility can feel like a rollercoaster ride for different professions.

Consider sales reps who can bunny-hop across industries with relative ease. But for the more specialized crowd, they're often left staring at the daunting cliffs of obsolescence and retraining costs.

But before we all run off and form an anti-competition support group, let's remember it's not all rain clouds. Yes, free competition might increase the risk of your skills becoming as obsolete as a floppy disk, but it also opens up new opportunities for human capital investment. More often than not, the balance tilts towards the latter. And let's not forget, the waves of technology and demographics might have a bigger hand in shaping human capital than competition.

So, wrapping things up, while democracy might throw a spanner in the works when it comes to returns on human capital and social mobility, it's not the big bad wolf in the inequality tale. The stuttering 'social elevator' of education in some swanky democracies might raise a few eyebrows, but laying the blame at democracy's doorstep is a tad unfair. At the end of the day, it's our friend representative democracy that drives the quest for equal opportunities - a cornerstone in the edifices of both meritocracy and democracy.

Multiculturalism and democracy

Let's start by narrowly defining

multiculturalism as significant differences based on ethnicity or religion, conveniently shelving geographical or ideological rivalries for now.

At first glance, one might surmise that multiculturalism and democracy are a bit like oil and water - they don't mix. After all, people often rally around single-issue parties defined by ethnic or religious identities. But hold on a minute, reality begs to differ.

Take a gander at India, a vast tapestry of multiculturalism woven into a democratic form. Here, you've got 20% of the population practicing a faith other than Hinduism, cohabitation of over 700 tribes, and a cacophony of 18 official languages spoken by 450 linguistic groups. And still, democracy stands.

However, as we cast our eyes towards smaller multicultural nations like Syria and Iraq, we see them torn apart by civil strife. Then, you have the totalitarian cocktail of multiculturalism that is China - a country where less than half of the population practices Shenism-Taoism and Buddhism among the Han Chinese. Yet, it's home to 55 official ethnic groups conversing in 292 languages, Mandarin only being the national language, with regional tongues like Cantonese also holding official status.

So, what gives? Why does multiculturalism comfortably sit with democracy, tolerance, and diversity in some places, and not others?

One argument points towards an overarching cultural inheritance, often rooted in the leadership of independence movements. For instance, in India, the firm hand of Gandhi's party - the National Congress Party - steadied the democratic helm for the first quarter-century of independence.

What makes India's democratic journey intriguing is how it survived the seismic shift from party dominance to a vibrant mix of smaller regional and ethnic parties, sometimes even being governed by a coalition of 14 parties. Democracy didn't crumble, it adapted.

A multitude of factors played a part in this outcome, but key among them was the choice of a federal system of government, the establishment of a unified and independent judicial system, and the acceptance of coalition governments in lieu of the traditional two-party rotation system.

For anyone in the European Union who's tempted to take a leap towards political union, I'd advise them to take a leaf out of India's book and give these factors a good, hard think.

8 Democracy in War and Peace

Brace yourselves for a thrilling waltz through the highs and lows of democracies during both peacetime bliss and the gut-wrenching turbulence of conflict. Let's kick things off with the 'peace dividend', a rather romantic name for the hefty pile of perks democracies bag when they choose chit-chat over cataclysm. This chapter cheekily titled 'Democracy's Peace Dividend' won't shy away from picking apart the knotty ties between peace-loving democracies and the sociopolitical bounty they could harvest.

We'll then swap our dancing shoes for combat boots, marching into the murkier realms of 'Civil Wars'. Here, we'll scrutinize how these fraternal feuds can shake up democracies, leaving a trail of human heartbreak and political pandemonium. We're laying out the dirty laundry – the triggers, the aftermath, and the could-have-beens, all while shining a spotlight on the crucial role democracies play in this chaotic drama.

The penultimate act, 'Nukes and Nutcases: The Democracy Conundrum', offers a front-row seat to the often-overlooked tussle between democratic principles and the haunting potential of apocalyptic choices. Democracy, for all its merits, can sometimes be like a dodgy flea market - everyone has a stall, including those peddling disaster. This 'democracy-for-all' paradox isn't just a head-scratcher, it's a Pandora's box we'll dare to open.

Finally, we'll take a detour to the land of vodka and Matryoshka dolls in 'Russian Riddles: Two Decades of Fear and Loathing'. This section lifts the iron curtain on the tense love-hate relationship between democracy, paranoia, power and the yearning for stability. Russia, with its roller-coaster ride through history, serves up a hearty helping of insights into the sometimes messy, often convoluted dynamics of democracy in times of serenity and storm.

So join us on this odyssey through the tempestuous seas of democracy. We'll be celebrating victories, mourning defeats, and asking the uncomfortable questions, all in the name of better understanding the complex, sometimes bewildering, world of democratic societies.

Democracy's peace dividend

You do not need to go back to 1795 and Kant's theory on Perpetual Peace: A Philosophical Sketch. Think of democracy as a device to restrict the predatory nature of humankind. This should prevent most wars, shouldn't it? On the contrary, dictatorship breeds predatory behaviour out of its need to always find external enemies and ultimately ending up in conflict and war. So, it is logical to expect a dividend from investing in democracy.

"Democracy, the beacon of peace," is an idea many of us love to cling onto. It's a comforting thought, isn't it? And why not? There's a good deal of brainy empirical research backing up the claim that democracies, with their peace-loving and human rights-championing ways, don't get into fisticuffs with each other. So, logically, if we stick a 'Welcome to the Democratic Club' sign on more countries, we should be looking at a world less marred by wars. A compelling argument, until recent years took this tidy theory, gave it a good shake, and sent it headfirst into the turbulent waters of the world's geopolitical reality.

Let's paint a picture of the world stage. It's not a pretty sight. Local and regional conflicts are sprouting up like weeds, and democracies, with their capes and principles, feel obliged to jump into the fray. Take the Russian-Ukrainian drama, for example. Russia struts in and invades Ukraine, leaving NATO and the global democratic league scrambling to react, and suddenly we're witnessing a surge in conventional weaponry. Not exactly the peaceful picture democracies are supposed to paint, is it?

And now, the million-dollar question: in such situations, should democracies don the gloves, face down the invaders, and attempt to gift-wrap democracy for them? Or is it enough to coax Russia, and other overambitious nations, back behind their borders? The answer could have ripples far beyond the immediate spat, giving food for thought to dictatorships and dictators-in-the-making, especially those in the 'we're big and important' BRICS group.

Let's take a look at China - currently sporting the title of the world's strongest dictatorship.

There's a growing buzz that China might have its eyes set on Taiwan, a democratically governed gem birthed by the leaders the Chinese communists showed the door. This isn't a rerun of the Soviet empire's downfall; it's a whole new ball game that needs a different playbook.

The global political climate is like a game of Jenga - fraught, unpredictable, and an arms race looking more and more like an inevitable tumble. This brings to the fore the critical need for democracies to flex their military muscles. After all, without military clout, how can democracies ensure their survival, especially when some home-grown pacifist movements might just be puppets on an authoritarian string?

Does that mean democracies should strip these groups of their democratic rights? Of course not. But a good dose of scrutiny of their activities and a loudspeaker to counteract any propaganda wouldn't go amiss. It's about maintaining the democratic tightrope act, preserving peace while protecting national interests.

Democracy's 'peace dividend' seems like a jigsaw puzzle with too many missing pieces in the current world order. As democracies navigate these choppy waters, the real worth of the 'peace dividend' will be gauged by the balancing act between military might and safeguarding democratic ideals. It's less about reducing wars, and more about peace that doesn't come at the cost of democratic principles.

In a nutshell, the 'peace dividend' is a high-wire act - a delicate dance between global peace, national security, and upholding democracy's cornerstone values. It demands a sharp eye on the world's power dynamics, an unflinching defence of democratic rights, and strategic responses. The path is filled with potholes and tripwires, but if we manage to get to the end, the payoff - a peaceful, democratic world - will have been worth the struggle.

Civil wars

The crumbling edifice of empires and the euphemistically termed 'decolonization' have invariably ignited a series of civil wars worldwide. Let's be clear, these newly freed nations, breaking the iron chains of colonization, quickly turned into a simmering cauldron of power tussles. With the

Cold War as a moody backdrop, our friendly giants - the USA and USSR - indulged in some puppetry from afar, using these novice nations as pawns in their global chessboard.

Yet, let's not forget, the collapse of the Soviet Union didn't sprinkle magic dust to make civil wars disappear. Instead, they hung around, rather impolitely, and even had the audacity to multiply. The Peace Research Institute Oslo (PRIO) gives us a stark snapshot - conflicts and wars per year, since 1990, oscillating between 30 and 56, peaking rather morosely in 2022. Add to this the rather harrowing death toll swinging annually between 25,000 and 140,000, hitting an apogee in 1991.

A fair chunk of these conflicts can be traced back to the vacuum left behind by the Soviet Union's dissolution. As if on cue, Russian mercenary groups popped up, eager beavers looking to make a quick buck from African nations previously under the Soviet umbrella. Operating under the guise of independence, these groups, wading through the murkiness of international law, fanned the flames of instability and fueled conflicts.

Just when you thought things couldn't get

messier, enter Islamic fundamentalist terrorism - a novel character in the drama of civil wars. Bankrolled by some generous Middle Eastern nations, these extremist elements added fuel to the already raging fire. While the age-old tug-of-war over natural resources still triggers many civil wars, this new breed of ethnically or religiously driven conflicts call for a fresh playbook for conflict resolution and peacekeeping.

Here's the conundrum: how does multiparty democracy survive in nations teetering on ethnic or religious divides? Do we stick a "one-size-fits-all" multicultural label on them and hope it sticks? Or perhaps consider more tailored dual government systems, similar to the intra-country state and regional governance structures? These questions aren't for show; they need proper chewing over if we are to stand a chance of mitigating civil wars and nurturing long-lasting peace.

In a nutshell, the post-colonial world, despite its lofty promises of self-determination and independence, has been bedeviled by a haunting surge in civil wars. These conflicts, spurred on by power dynamics, economic opportunism, and the rising tide of ethnic and religious divides, pose a serious challenge to global peace and stability. Tackling these challenges calls for a sophisticated, context-sensitive approach that factors in the unique cultural, ethnic, and religious tapestry of these nations. It's only with this understanding that we can hope to staunch the flow of civil wars and champion a more peaceful, democratic world.

Democracy conundrum: Nukes and nutcases

The global landscape is now pockmarked with a new breed of hazards, such as nuclear weapons, and other weapons of mass destruction (WMDs) looming large. They present an unnerving Pandora's box of challenges, not merely for democratic nations, but indeed, for all human beings on this blue planet. It's like sitting on the edge of a cliff, gazing into an abyss.

Once upon a time, the world had a failsafe: Mutually Assured Destruction (MAD). The logic was straightforward, bordering on quaint: if a nuclear war could wipe us all out, then no nation in its right mind would ever light the fuse. But what happens when sanity isn't a given?

The arrival of so-called "strategic" nuclear weapons in the arsenals of not-so-stable regimes is a ticking time bomb. The trouble here isn't the hardware; it's the human element. Can we trust an unhinged autocrat or a zealous theocracy not to plunge headlong into collective suicide? It's a sobering thought. Even a Putin, now more feeble than fierce, doesn't inspire confidence in rational decision-making.

So, what's the way out? The world community, irrespective of their political hues, must come together to enforce collective controls on these deadly toys. In a nutshell, the red button shouldn't be within the reckless reach of one man or a clique, but should come under a broader, more accountable decision-making framework.

The placement of such lethal arsenals in outer space or the dawn of new, unthinkable weapons requires a shared global agreement. The militarization of space or unchecked WMD innovation can push us into an apocalyptic arms race that could make doomsday movies look like child's play.

But let's be clear: these are just Band-Aids. The real cure lies in a more wholesale global shift towards democratic governance. Why? Because democracies, with their built-in emphasis on the rule of law, human rights, and collective decision-making, provide a bulwark against the irresponsible use of WMDs.

In light of this, the battle for democracy transcends the quest for political rights and freedoms. It morphs into a struggle for survival, a fight to avert the end-of-days scenarios that a nuclear war would bring about. The dogged pursuit of democratic values, therefore, gains paramount significance in a world teetering on the edge of nuclear horror.

So here's the bottom line: the arms race and the spread of WMDs pose a life-or-death challenge to humanity. They underscore the pressing need for collective global decision-making, consensual rules on space militarization, and most crucially, the universal adoption of democracy. Such steps are not only key to warding off the specter of a nuclear war but are vital for the continued existence of our species. Thus, the fight for democracy morphs into an essential part of our shared mission for a safer, more peaceful world.

Russian riddles: Decades of Fear and Loathing

If you're seeking a masterclass in the erosion

of freedom under non-capitalist systems, look no further than post-communist Russia. With its unique brand of oligarchic state capitalism, it's a textbook study of how not to reform an economy. Now, I wouldn't dare to claim to be an expert on Russia - my encounters with the country have been limited to two brief visits, to Moscow in 1991 and to St. Petersburg in 2013.

In St. Petersburg, amidst the throngs in the Hermitage Museum, I found myself in a reflective mood. What struck me most wasn't the grandeur of the museum, but the city itself. Despite over 20 years of post-communism, the once imperial city was visibly decrepit, and its citizens dour and nationalistic. The selection of goods on sale - trinkets, amber, and an unhealthy dose of communist memorabilia - was painfully limited, as if time had stopped in its tracks.

I grew up under Salazar's authoritarian rule in Portugal, a system admired by President Putin, and could relate to the sense of fear, the yearning for past glories, and the collective disillusionment. It was palpable, etched on their faces, visible in their deference to authority.

I remember stepping into a souvenir shop, where a plaque still proudly announced it had been opened with a minister's special permission. At a restaurant, which was once a czarist palace and a

Soviet Trade Union headquarters, I was served a bland meal while a young violinist played mournful tunes. The setting was surreal, and it was abundantly clear - Russia's free enterprise was a mere façade.

Russia's economy, to put it bluntly, is as diverse as a loaf of bread. It's primarily hinged on arms and energy exports, with the latter forming almost 70% of its total exports. Combined with other commodities, these sectors make up around 50% of the federal government's tax revenue. In comparison to the Euro Area, Russia's exports are just a mere 15%.

Chrystia Freeland, in her book "Plutocrats", attempted to analyze the differences between Russia's oligarchs and China's communist party bosses. She argued that China's market reforms were slower, but its avenues for rent-seeking were more varied and less transparent. Yet, I find this explanation woefully inadequate.

To my mind, the striking difference lies in the level of international trade engagement. China embraced free trade regions and hastened its WTO membership, while Russia only met the WTO membership requirements in 2012. Couple this with a deep-seated disregard for small businesses, rampant corruption, and an atmosphere of fear, and you have a perfect recipe for stifling entrepreneurship.

In a nutshell, Russia's journey underscores the pivotal role freedom plays in fostering democracy and economic growth. Without it, fear creeps in - the fear of losing power among those in charge, and fear of losing security among the populace. This fear, if unchecked, invariably veers towards authoritarian nationalism, invoking the specter of social unrest or fabricated external threats.

Overcoming these fears requires genuine democracy and the relinquishment of predatory imperialism, an unpleasant vestige of the old KGB. Until then, Russia risks becoming an outcast, a pariah excluded from trading with the Western world. In essence, Russia is at a crossroads - it can either choose the path of fear or embrace the transformative power of freedom. Only time will tell which path it chooses.

9 Political Ideology and Democracy

Imagine a world buzzing with political ideologies. They're everywhere, and they're shaping the rules of the game for all societies. Now, take democracy, a common thread that runs through them all. Democracy is all about fairness, rights, and a voice for everyone. Our mission? To give you a crash course in how these ideologies shape democracy.

First up: "Individualism and Collectivism". A grand tug-of-war if you will. On one side, individualism champions personal freedom, mirroring liberal democracy. On the other side, collectivism roots for the group over the lone wolf, which brews a different flavour of democracy.

Next, we tackle the riddle of "Capitalism without Democracy?" Not all that glitters is gold, and not all capitalists are democrats. There are times when these strange bedfellows part ways, and we're going to dive into that intrigue.

Third on the agenda, we address the puzzling trajectory of "Why Socialism Often Ends-Up in Dictatorship". Sure, socialism waves the flag for equality, but has a knack for ending up in dictatorship. We'll dissect this political enigma, looking for the missing links between socialist ideals and democratic reality.

Then, we grapple with "Theocracies and Democracy". A sticky wicket, this. When religion takes the reins, can democracy really get a fair shake? We're diving into the challenges of this often-uneasy cohabitation.

Lastly, let's talk about a special breed of 'independents' who strut around the political arena with their noses in the air, seem to believe that political parties should prostrate themselves, seeking their favour. Should they?

This chapter is your fast-track guide through the maze of political ideologies and their relationships with democracy. We're peeling back layers, and hopefully, clearing some of the fog off the political landscape. Buckle up.

Individualism and collectivism

Capitalism's odd couple: Keynes vs. Hayek. If the political spectrums had a frenemy couple, Keynes and Hayek would be it. Their tug-of-war is the bedrock of capitalism's boundaries today, drawing lines between the liberal (or 'socialist' for our European friends) and libertarian ends of the spectrum. Fast forward to today, and their masterpiece texts, Hayek's "Road to Serfdom" (1944) and Keynes's "General Theory" (1936), remain must-reads for any political devotee.

Now, these two were quite the pair - contemporaries in time, but poles apart in ideas. Yet, they maintained a bromance that outlived their ideological skirmishes. Hayek admitted, with charming candor, "We disagreed aplenty, but never stopped being chums". Even Keynes was a fanboy of Hayek's work, once gushing, "It's a cracking good read…I find myself nodding along, quite moved, in fact."

Their shared fan club for market capitalism and economic liberalism was a love they both confessed. But fast forward to today, and their followers are acting more like feuding religious zealots, each convinced their 'prophet' had the exclusive hotline to truth. They've forgotten that

Keynes and Hayek, like fans of the Abrahamic religions, were singing from the same hymn sheet - they just harmonized differently.

Both gents championed economic liberalism, built on good old-fashioned, 19th century individualism. And no, we're not talking about the selfie-taking, ego-boosting individualism of today. The duo appreciated individualism for its triple threat: it guarded personal liberty, boosted efficiency, and preserved life's wonderful variety. Hayek, ever the philosopher, saw individualism as a humbling nod to the superior forces shaping reason. For him, collective control or social planning were akin to a ham-fisted karaoke singer butchering a beautiful melody.

So where did the dynamic duo part ways? The devil, as they say, is in the details. Their beef revolved around the business cycle and the push-pull of individualism and collectivism. Keynes was ready to throw individualism under the bus for full employment. Hayek, on the other hand, wasn't buying it. He feared this would pave the road to a society-wide control freak show.

Rather than launching into a West Side Story rumble, perhaps followers of Keynes and Hayek should take a breather. They might find more fruitful work exploring the contours of their theories, figuring out where they apply best. After all, it's what their 'prophets' probably would've wanted.

A marriage of convenience?

Capitalism and democracy, inseparable BFFs or an awkward pairing? If we're talking the real deal - market capitalism - they're two peas in a pod. Competition and free markets are the driving force of capitalism, just like democracy needs a hearty serving of freedom for good governance and rule of law. It's no wonder the two are often seen as a package deal.

Yet, you'll find skeptics on both ends of the political spectrum. Some, on a misguided understanding of both systems; others, well, just don't like the outcome.

Let's talk about democracy - "government of the people, by the people, for the people". It's about majority rule with representatives chosen by us but balanced with respect for the rights of minorities. Sounds simple, right?

But there are alternatives - the totalitarian and authoritarian flavours of government. Totalitarian regimes are all about absolute power, underpinned by some dogmatic ideology or religion, with opposition stamped out in no uncertain terms. Authoritarian regimes? They're totalitarian-lite - less ideological, a tad more freedom, as long as the status quo isn't threatened.

Past offenders? Nazi Germany, Stalin's USSR. Current culprits? Look no further than North Korea and Saudi Arabia. Now, where to place countries like Iran, Russia, or China on this scale is a hot potato. These regimes, while not overtly anti-capitalist, can be capitalism's cheerleaders when it suits them.

We can measure a regime's evolution with two simple tools - the state's involvement in the economy and citizens' freedoms under the rule of law. Strong leaders and single-party dominance don't necessarily rule these out, but beware, elites who dislike competition can become a sticky fixture.

Liberalism can be a crucial antidote, helping keep both capitalism and democracy healthy. It's a curious parallel that democracy and capitalism face similar governance challenges. Imagine, if you will, voters as shareholders, political parties as asset managers, parliament as the board of directors, and government as executive officers. The parallels are striking and so are the challenges — representation, self-perpetuating elites, and attempts to skew voting rights.

To sum up, capitalism and democracy may not be joined at the hip, but they've got a cosy mutual reinforcement thing going on. Step away from one, and you're not just disturbing the peace, but risk flirting with a perverse form of capitalism. Let's just say, it's a relationship worth keeping an eye on.

From socialism to dictatorship: A slippery slope?

It seems almost uncanny, doesn't it? How socialist regimes, regardless of their mode of ascension - revolution or ballot box, seem to morph into authoritarian or totalitarian personas.

The revolutionary route to dictatorship is fairly obvious - the revolutionaries just don't want to let go. However, the enigma lies in those democratically elected socialists who promised a fair dance, yet tangoed into non-democratic regimes.

There are two paths to this transformation. The first, an evolution into communism. It starts with socialism's fluffy pro-democracy ideals, but the path to communism demands a rather hard pivot towards a dictatorship of the proletariat, endearingly rebranded as 'popular democracy'.

In the 19th century, some already predicted the degeneration of socialism into something nastier. For example, Bastiat in his book 'The Law' warned that men would plunder if it proved easier than working and once in power, they'd set up a system of reprisals against other classes. A century later, Schumpeter, pessimistic about human nature, predicted capitalism would devolve into corporatism, making way for socialism.

Thankfully, history's silver lining shows that socialism doesn't always go full-on totalitarian. Sometimes, it downshifts to social democracy, accepting capitalism's place at the table. The Scandinavian model demonstrates this shift, but it must be a substantial pivot or the regime risks capsizing.

There's a second way socialism can cling on in a democracy, let's call it 'Latin American Populism'. Venezuela provides the blueprint here. Hugo Chavez swept to power on the back of impoverished masses, keenly "bribed" with state-sponsored social programs paid for by the middle class and by squeezing the country's natural resources for his cronies.

This model, however, has a nasty habit of self-combusting. The economic inefficiency becomes so great that not even the squandering of huge natural resources can mask the decline. And the demands on the welfare state escalate with each new handout, leading to a fiscal nosedive.

Such symptoms are glaringly apparent in Venezuela. Facing growing opposition, the socialist rulers have clamped down with a litany of prohibitions, incarcerations, and persecutions to keep their grip on power.

So, what's the prognosis? It seems socialism, despite its democratic origins, has a way of landing democracy in limbo. The only escape routes seem to be a U-turn towards social democracy or a leap of faith into the cold embrace of state capitalism, communism, or dictatorship.

Theocracies and democracy

Divine democracy? Navigating the waters of theocracies and democracies. Picture a family reunion of political regimes - you'd find everyone from the well-dressed democracies to the sombre theocracies and an array of monarchies and republics making small talk over the buffet. The political world is nothing short of a bustling gathering, with each member showcasing its quirks moulded by history, culture, and societal influences.

The fascinating pair of the theocracies and democracies, for example, is a conversation starter. Theocracies, with their divine staff of command, bring religious leaders onto the political stage. Democracies, conversely, hand the microphone to the people, enabling them to choose their leaders and steer the national policy ship. They seem to be speaking different languages, but their conversation isn't as discordant as you might think.

Imagine a theocracy trying its hand at democracy. It could work, provided it doesn't trample on religious freedom and ensures its religious leaders are answerable to the ballot box. This peculiar arrangement is visible in some Western democracies which, although predominantly secular, sport religious accessories. The United Kingdom takes it a step further, with the monarch moonlighting as the head of the Anglican Church - a blending of roles that turns heads in both religious and political circles.

Yet, religion and politics make for a slippery dance floor, and the dance becomes even more treacherous when religious doctrines take a radical turn, veering the system towards intolerance and sectarianism. Consider Iran, Israel, and the swelling Evangelical influence in American politics as prime examples of this precarious dance.

Iran's theocratic republic has the religious leaders in the driver's seat, a situation which has often put the brakes on civil liberties. Here, radical religious ideologies seem to bulldoze democratic values, turning the democratic dream into a mirage.

Israel, while not a pure theocracy, has intertwined its political identity with the concept of a Jewish state so closely that it's hard to tell where one ends and the other begins. The friction between religious and secular Jews, as well as between Jews and Arabs, underlines the struggle of a religious state to uphold the democratic pillars of equality and inclusivity.

In the United States, the rise of Evangelical influence has sparked questions about the line that separates the church from the state, despite the country's secular democratic constitution. It's akin to finding a religious hymn book in a democratic library - out of place and a tad controversial.

These instances highlight that theocratic regimes tiptoeing on democratic grounds often risk a fall. Religious zeal, if unchecked, can chip away at the bedrock of democratic principles, spawning intolerance, and autocracy.

In conclusion, theocracies and democracies are distinctive guests at the political party, each sporting unique conversation topics and dance moves. They can share the dance floor, but striking the right rhythm - one that respects religious beliefs without compromising democratic values - requires finesse and constant adjustment, particularly with the fervent religious passion often ready to hijack the beat.

While theocratic states can pull off a democratic dance, the potential missteps they pose might suggest a preference for a secular DJ. This doesn't mean banning religious tunes from the playlist, but rather ensuring they don't drown out the democratic melodies of equality, inclusivity, and the rule of law. The dance between theocracies and democracy is a complex tango, reminding us that the quest for the perfect rhythm of governance continues to make political feet tap.

Independence: A veil for opportunism

Picture this: a fresh-off-the-boat government claiming to have a third of its cabinet as 'independents'. This triggers the proverbial thumbs-up from some, while others slap their foreheads in disbelief. To weigh the pros and cons of these so-called independents, we first need to dissect what on earth an 'independent' actually is.

The term 'independent' in politics is as slippery as an eel. Depending on who you ask, it could mean a party-neutral sage, an apolitical alien, a chameleon (cosying up to the ruling party), or even a downright anti-politics activist.

All these definitions, while colourful, are a bit like trying to pin the tail on the donkey – they're hopelessly wide of the mark. An 'independent', in its purest sense, is simply a person not wearing any party's badge. Period. Considering the abysmal party affiliation numbers in Portugal (trailing behind even football clubs), it appears most of us are accidental independents. This is why labelling someone as an 'independent' is about as useful as a chocolate teapot when assessing their worth.

Let's clear one thing up: our stance towards political parties isn't the same as our position on politics. One of the perks of representative democracy is that you don't need to be a political junkie to have a say. Come election day, your personal, non-exchangeable vote lets you make your mark without having to dive deep into the politics pool.

But for those with a fondness for politics, it's a different story. Like it or not, they'll have some sort of entanglement with political parties. This can range from die-hard activists and card-carrying members, through to influential or fair-weather supporters, sympathisers, frequent and sporadic voters, all the way to adversaries, critics, dislikers, or those who just couldn't care less about a political party. Thus, it's a head-scratcher when people mix up independence with impartiality or indifference.

Let me take a leaf out of my own book. As a cheerleader for constitutional liberalism, I find myself occasionally tossing my vote in PSD's direction, even though they give off strong social-democratic vibes that I can't quite jive with. I'm not on their membership roster, but that doesn't slap an 'independent' label on me, not if it implies being indifferent or impartial to their election results. Similarly, I might not be a football fanatic, but given a choice between Porto and Benfica, I'd be waving the Porto flag. So, when both are on the pitch, I'm rooting for Porto. Clearly, I'm not indifferent to the match's outcome. That's right, I'm not an 'independent' in the sense of being impartial.

Ponder this: claiming that Dr. Catorga or Dr. Silva Lopes are independent of the PSD and PS respectively, isn't a declaration of their indifference towards these parties. The former is a PSD influence peddler, while the latter occasionally hoped onto the PS bandwagon. But just because they don't tote their respective party membership cards, it doesn't mean they're sitting on the fence when it comes to party policies or yawning at their political shenanigans.

The million-dollar question then is, why on earth do these folks not officially tie the knot with their respective parties? Morally speaking, there are both commendable and dodgy reasons for evading the party affiliation tag, even if these same individuals don't shirk from holding elected or non-elected political posts.

For those who regularly swing a party's way but don't fancy diving headlong into the political fray, there are plenty of valid excuses. Maybe they prefer their independence, free from the shackles of party discipline. Perhaps they can't stomach internal power struggles, or just don't have enough hours in the day for party duties. Or it could be that they're not fired up enough for the rough and tumble of political life.

However, lurking in the shadows are morally questionable motivations – the political equivalent of playing the field. Think of those who dodge party membership to keep their options open for juicy political posts from other parties. Or mayors who'd rather stay unaffiliated to rope in the support of foot soldiers from various parties for their re-election bid.

Sure, there may be cases where such political

shenanigans can be shrugged off, but in others, it's a blatant case of opportunism that's nothing short of a slap in the face. Take, for instance, the unelected political office bearers at the national level who, sensing a change in political winds, suddenly turn into critics of the status quo, while cooing sweet nothings about opposition policies. The goal? To keep their seat warm or land a cushy reappointment when the government changes. This chameleon-like behaviour is especially prominent among the cheerleaders of the 'centrão' and those bound by familial ties, friendships, or mutual interests.

Let's talk about a special breed of 'independents' who strut around the political arena with a haughty swagger, purporting to be high and mighty, either above the fray of party politics or simply indifferent to it. These individuals, with their noses in the air, seem to believe that political parties should prostrate themselves, seeking their favour. Such arrogance, if not merely the sublimation of their weakness, is a virulent strain of opportunism that's highly toxic to the body politic.

Cutting to the chase, the instances where independent status is hijacked for dubious and morally reprehensible reasons far outweigh the legitimate ones. Therefore, one struggles to see the value in glorifying the label of 'independent' as a boon for political life. Political parties should focus on casting their nets wider, drawing in non-member supporters for political positions (even if it means roping in fair-weather friends), rather than elevating the status of 'independent' as something desirable. The spoils of such a strategy, in terms of competence, are often dwarfed by the surge in opportunism.

Those in political office ought to wear their political affiliations on their sleeves, and if they make a habit of assuming political posts, it would be only fitting for them to make their political leanings official through party membership. Transparency in such matters is not just a boon for the individual and the party but is also the lifeblood of democracy.

In a truly representative democracy, transparency isn't optional. In its absence, especially in a country like ours where unelected political positions are a dime a dozen, there's a real risk of blurring the lines between representative democracy and the twisted versions one might encounter in Latin American countries, à la Mexico or Venezuela. We certainly wouldn't want our democracy going down that rabbit hole, would we?

10 Threats to Democracy

Strap yourselves in for an eye-popping roller-coaster ride as we delve into the seedier side of democracy. It's a twilight journey through the chills of chaos, tyrant takeovers, rogue leadership, far-right fanaticism, corruption quicksteps, public opinion puppeteering, and the head-spinning waltz of globalization. All of these are not just bogeymen under democracy's bed but very real adversaries in the political arena.

Our first act, 'The Risk of Chaos for Democracy', throws us into a riotous carnival where democracy is at risk of losing its footing amid the frenzy. Here, we'll examine the tightrope democracies tread and the not-so-fun fairground ride that ensues when balance is lost.

'The Overturn of Elected Representatives by Dictators' is a thrilling game of thrones, recounting the disturbing tales of democracies pulled from their pedestals by iron-fisted usurpers. This isn't a spooky bedtime story; it's yesterday's headlines and potentially tomorrow's.

In 'The Election of Nuts and Dictators:

Trump - Caligula or Incitatus?' we play a political game of 'Would You Rather?' with a larger-than-life reality TV star turned president and a loony Roman Emperor with a horse for a senator. It's an uncanny round of democracy's bizarre version of pin the tail on the donkey.

Our tour through 'The Bumpy Road of Democracy: Tackling the Far Right' veers into the gravelly path of radical ideologies and their jarring challenge to democratic ideals. 'Corruption and Democracy: A Tango of Complexity' unveils a dance-off where democracy and corruption try to lead, often tripping over each other's feet.

Onto 'Democracy and the Manipulation of Public Opinion', we uncover the age-old magic trick of pulling public sentiment from a hat, a game that has the power to twist democratic processes into unrecognizable shapes.

Finally, 'Globalization vs Democracy: A Tangled Affair' throws us into a messy tug-of-war between global strings and local reins.

This chapter invites you to a topsy-turvy political carnival, full of spectacles that threaten to derail the democratic process. Through this, we hope to unmask these threats and perhaps learn how to tame the democracy's wild ride.

The risk of chaos for democracy

Imagine democracy and capitalism as conjoined twins, each thriving off the other. Now, like the secret sauce in your favourite burger, liberalism is the ingredient that keeps this duo intact. Historically, liberal parties have been like the heart of capitalist societies—pumping out balanced governance and celebrating individual freedoms. But a glance at today's political climate and you'd think we've landed on an alien planet, with liberal ideals gradually sliding into obscurity. That's like taking the secret sauce out of your burger, leaving us with a tasteless political sandwich. Add a sprinkle of societal chaos to the mix and voila, we have a recipe for a democracy disaster.

Liberalism's slow dance into the shadows is primarily due to a growing opposition to capitalism. Picture two feisty dogs (socialist and communist ideologies from the left, and nationalist and corporatist perspectives from the right) tugging at the same bone (capitalism). This tug-of-war threatens to tilt the scale, creating a hotbed for societal unrest and potential chaos.

History is littered with instances where chaos has opened the doors to dictatorships. The fall of the Roman Empire and the French Revolution's turbulent period are glaring examples of this unnerving trend. Chaos acts like a demolition crew, pulling apart the social contract, crippling institutions, and setting up a stage for opportunistic demagogues to grab the reins of power.

However, let's not paint all societal disruptions with the same brush. Not all are the death knell for democracy. Take, for instance, France, which has weathered significant social disruptions in May 1968 and July 2023 without letting its democratic roots wither. The secret? A careful, measured restoration of public order and keeping the military and police forces on a political leash.

Here's a common but dangerous myth: the road to public order is paved with military boots. History, as evidenced by el-Sisi's Egypt, tells us otherwise. Military rule often serves as a launchpad for dictators, thereby posing a grave danger to democracy.

In the eye of the chaos storm, maintaining the continuity of democratic institutions is as vital as a lighthouse in a raging sea. These institutions, even when under pressure, provide an anchor of stability and reassurance to the public. They uphold the rule of law, protect civil liberties, and prevent political power from being a monopoly game. So, come rain or shine, keeping democratic institutions intact is a must.

Averting the risk of chaos calls for a deep dive into the root causes of social unrest. It's about bridging economic divides, fighting systemic corruption, and ensuring that the rule of law isn't merely a fancy phrase. Plus, let's not forget the role of education in this drama. It's a potent tool to bolster democratic norms and nurture a culture of civic participation. When citizens grasp the value of democracy and the peril of authoritarianism, they're less likely to cheer for a dictatorial regime.

To sum up, the spectre of chaos looms large over democracy, particularly in the light of dwindling liberal principles. Safely navigating societal upheaval requires a careful balance of maintaining public order and preserving democratic norms and institutions. This demands a steadfast commitment to liberal principles, unwavering civic education, and a staunch resistance to the allure of temporary military rule. Only by tackling these challenges head-on can we shield our democratic systems, ensuring they weather even the roughest storms.

Overturn of elected representatives by dictators

Imagine democracy as a shiny new smartphone: full of promise, touted as life-changing, but susceptible to hacks and malicious viruses. More specifically, imagine a scenario where the phone's very operating system turns rogue, hijacking its function. Sounds frightening, doesn't it? That's precisely the scenario we confront when we talk about dictators coming to power by exploiting democratic systems.

Flick back through history's dusty pages, and you'll find Germany, 1930s, staring back at you, with Adolf Hitler taking the spotlight. The Weimar Republic then was like a shaky tower of Jenga blocks, one false move away from tumbling. Hitler, canny as a fox and backed by the National Socialist Party, sniffed out this vulnerability. His ticket to power wasn't some military coup but democracy itself, cleverly using fear as his campaign slogan. But the moment he set foot in office, Hitler took democracy to the cleaners, swapping it for a totalitarian regime faster than you can say 'autocracy'. This grim chapter in history offers a stark reminder: desperate times might birth an illusion of strength and decisiveness, which, if not checked, can quickly veer into a dictatorial nightmare.

Fast-forward to more recent times, and we find Russia under Vladimir Putin's rule. Instead of a dramatic seizure of power, Putin's path was more akin to boiling a frog slowly; the poor creature doesn't realise it's being cooked until it's too late. Putin, the chef in this scenario, methodically chipped away at democratic institutions, all while maintaining a façade of democracy. The man has turned quashing opposition, controlling media, and rigging elections into an art form, ensuring his iron grip on power remains unchallenged. This example is a chilling reminder that democracies can die not only from violent coups but also from a steady, sinister erosion of its foundational pillars.

Speaking of reminders, let's not forget the time when the United States had a hair-raising brush with a potential constitutional crisis on January 6, 2021. If it weren't for the resilience of the democratic system and the robust checks and balances in place, the Capitol invasion could have spiraled out of control faster than a trending Twitter hashtag.

But robust systems alone won't cut the mustard. Democracy needs its citizens to be as alert and informed as a sentry on night watch. A healthy democracy isn't just about voting; it's about understanding the nuances of democratic systems, spotting signs of authoritarianism creeping in like fog on a cold morning and being aware of the power and danger of a free press.

Let's not forget the crucial role international allies play in this saga. Much like friends who warn you against a bad investment, global institutions and alliances are vital in applying pressure on dictatorial regimes and championing democratic forces within troubled nations.

In conclusion, the phenomenon of dictators ousting elected representatives is as real as the nose on your face and as menacing as a ticking time bomb. To prevent such democratic upsets, we need systems that are as sturdy as a veteran's resolve, citizens who are as vigilant as a hawk, and global cooperation that matches a symphony orchestra's harmony. In a world teeming with challenges and threats, the task of preserving and strengthening our democratic institutions isn't just important—it's a dire necessity.

Trump: Caligula or Incitatus?

Ever been caught between a rock and a hard place? Imagine that rock being the emperor Caligula, the infamously sadistic tyrant who reportedly doted on his horse Incitatus so much, he made it a senator. Picture the hard place as Incitatus, who despite being a literal horse, had a posh marble stable, purple blankets, and a snazzy gem-studded collar - not to mention a senate seat.

Now replace Caligula with Donald Trump and Incitatus with the GOP, and you've got yourself a political sitcom. Trump, a reality show star and man known for slapping his name on buildings, somehow found himself as the Republican candidate for the most powerful position in the world. It begs the question: was Trump the GOP's own Incitatus, or was he more of a Caligula, turning the GOP into his personal Incitatus?

Political comedies aside, the sobering reality is that voters often elect outliers as a sort of protest against the political status quo. Putting a joker in charge could provide a break from the humdrum if the nation wasn't instrumental to global peace or if the new head honcho didn't come with a baggage of risky ideas. But this isn't a sitcom, and neither the U.S. is an insignificant player on the world stage, nor Trump a leader devoid of dicey convictions summarised in the table below.

Trump position	Plain English Translation
PAY FOR THE WALL	A stupid and inefficient way of fighting illegal immigrants and drug dealers while creating a conflict with Mexico.
HEALTHCARE REFORM	Dismantle Obamacare and leave millions without health cover.
U.S.-CHINA TRADE REFORM	Destroy world trade and create unnecessary and dangerous hostility with China
VETERANS ADMINISTRATION REFORMS	Increase military spending.
TAX REFORM	Tax cuts for the wealthy.
SECOND AMENDMENT RIGHTS	Support the gun lobby.
IMMIGRATION REFORM	Persecute immigrants

His catchphrase, Make America Great Again, is a lot less glamorous when you unpack it. It might topple the Dollar, shake the U.S. economy, reduce America's global leadership, and become a threat to world peace. His nationalist, xenophobic, homophobic, and militaristic stance has the potential to push allies away, foster divisions within the country, and stir up new enemies. The century-old vision of America as a beacon for democracy, fairness and opportunity could take a serious hit.

I almost couldn't believe that Americans would vote such a candidate into the presidency, but they did. Hence, we're faced with the possibility that Trump is both a modern-day Caligula and his own Incitatus. Of course, the American system is equipped with checks and balances, and thankfully, Trump hasn't managed to fulfill his entire agenda.

The fact that a robust democracy like America could make such a choice isn't all that shocking, especially considering some weariness with a self-perpetuating political class. But if Americans choose to elect him again, their faith in democracy as the best system to choose the best leaders could crumble. Making a mistake once is human, twice is forgivable, but three times? Well, that's just daft.

We must then consider what democratic remedies are available to counter such misguided choices.

Bumpy road to democracy: The far right

The kerfuffle over whether Marine Le Pen of the National Front should join the anti-terrorism rally in Paris throws into sharp relief a popular democratic blind spot. The question – should we put up with parties that lean towards xenophobia and a whiff of totalitarianism in our democracy? – has an answer that's as plain as day: Absolutely! Unless, of course, we're content with a half-baked version of democracy.

Now, there's one string attached here. These

parties need to play nice, eschewing violence and sticking to the democratic rulebook. It's the same rule for extreme left or extreme right, and their past misdemeanors don't alter the equation.

Personally, I've no doubt that if the National Front in France or the Communist Party in Portugal ever got to pull the political levers, they'd be quick to cook up a dictatorship, just to keep their hands on the power button. That's why I keep banging on about the dangers lurking in these so-called democratic parties with totalitarian leanings.

But let's not get ahead of ourselves. If anyone thought of giving the Portuguese Communist Party the boot, I'd be first in line, placard in hand, to protest for their right to freedom. After all, their freedom isn't a jot less valuable than mine.

In Portugal, when the PCP pulls the union strings to trigger public transport strikes, leaving us all in the lurch, I don't throw a fit at the PCP. I save my ire for the laws that let unions call strikes willy-nilly.

In the same vein, I don't point the finger at far-right and far-left radicals for their European upswing. The real culprits, in my book, are the democratic parties from both sides, who've lost the plot and alienated their voters. The real alarm bell ringing across Europe is the dwindling clout of moderate, reformist parties.

Corruption and democracy: A Tango

Dictatorships are generally corrupt, but democracies are not exempt from this plague. In the grand ballroom of global affairs, corruption and democracy have always been odd dance partners. They twirl in a bizarre ballet, their footwork leaving indelible marks on a nation's socio-economic canvas. The common assumption is that as the night of democracy advances, corruption slinks off, wilting in the growing light. But scholarly chatter suggests an entirely different choreography — an inverted U, if you will, where corruption initially prances proudly with nascent democracy, then, somewhat exhausted, retreats as the dance matures.

However, the dance isn't so straightforward. The routine includes a maddening myriad of moves: a deft deflection here, a hidden hand there. Democracy, by definition, should be corruption's natural nemesis. After all, its heart throbs with accountability, transparency, and participation — an antithesis to the shadowy dalliances of corruption. If democracy were a dance instructor, it would insist on a routine of transparency, an ensemble of accountability, and audience participation that would keep the dancers in line.

Yet, merely donning the attire of democracy doesn't necessarily keep corruption at bay. Much like in a dance, the quality of the steps matters more than the quantity. A casual glance around the global dance floor reveals this. Brazil and Greece, despite their enthusiastic twirls of representative democracy, often find themselves awkwardly stepping on the toes of corruption. Meanwhile, the likes of Singapore and the UAE, known for their more reserved dance styles, keep corruption at arm's length. This striking divergence underscores that other choreographers — institutional functioning, economic conditions, societal norms — have a say in the dance routine.

The number of times corruption and democracy change partners in the dance leaves us scratching our heads — an issue academics affectionately label 'endogeneity.' How do we measure democracy's influence on corruption when they're so intertwined in their dance routine? A novel approach suggests observing their conduct during times of conflict, considering democracies are seldom seen throwing punches at each other on the dance floor. Indeed, when this is taken into account, it appears democracy does lead to corruption off the floor more often than not.

When we turn our gaze to nations like Angola, Central African Republic, Republic of Congo, Guinea-Bissau, Mozambique, Nigeria, Somalia, Swaziland, Turkmenistan, Ukraine, and Uzbekistan, we can appreciate the subtle shifts in their dance routines, as they have made commendable strides in sidelining corruption. Yet, these nations, notorious for letting corruption take the lead, still lag on the global dance scorecard, the Absence of Corruption Index.

In this global dance-off, outliers are bound to catch the eye. The dance sequence between corruption and democracy is less a predictable waltz and more an improvisational jazz routine. Corruption's dance card is filled out by various partners, from politics to economy to culture, reminding us that pinning all our hopes on democracy as the solo performer in the fight against corruption is a naive overture.

In conclusion, democracy does indeed bring a unique rhythm to the floor, setting the tempo with transparency, accountability, and citizen participation. Yet, the corruption-democracy dance-off is far from a straightforward two-step. It's an intricate interplay contingent on the strength and quality of democratic moves, societal norms, and the presence of other dancers. Thus, to truly sweep corruption off its feet, we need to take into account all the factors that influence this delicate dance, not merely the democracy routine.

Democracy and public opinion manipulation

Consider Greece, the cradle of democracy, and the fact that the ancient Greeks were astute enough to realise that direct democracy needed to evolve into representative democracy. The motivations were clear then and remain so today - cost-effectiveness and the desire to avoid demagoguery. It's simply impractical and exorbitant to have every citizen involved in the creation, discussion, and approval of all legislation. Instead, elected representatives offer a more efficient solution, mirroring the views of various groups while being educated enough to avoid being swayed by beguiling speeches.

Now, let's turn the clock back to Aristotle and his attempt to regulate rhetoric in politics and law, seeking to move away from Plato's rather gloomy description of rhetoric as "the persuasion of ignorant masses within the courts and assemblies". Fast-forward to the 20th century, a period when the art of persuasion experienced a revival, thanks in no small part to progress in psychology.

Regrettably, this progress had its dark side,

manifesting in the manipulation of mass psychology. Certain political movements exploited this potent combination of rhetoric and psychology, using martial music and rallies to stir up hatred towards perceived or contrived enemies.

However, in democratic societies, this psychological knowledge was primarily employed for peaceful objectives, giving birth to the budding industry of advertising. Soon enough, politics too fell under its spell.

Yet, there's an even more insidious form of manipulation at play – public relations. PR tactics are more deceptive than advertising, as they often cloak the identities of their sponsors and their real intentions, using a network of unknowing opinion makers and groups to shape public perception. This ability to set up extravagant PR and advertising campaigns to deflect blame and manipulate the narrative gives certain organisations a disturbingly potent propaganda tool.

So, the million-dollar question is this - how does representative democracy navigate this maze of rhetoric, mass psychology, and the tools of advertising and PR? I propose a two-pronged strategy.

Firstly, inspired by Aristotle's insights, we

need to shine a light on these industries, particularly **PR**, and impose robust regulations when they're operating within the political sphere.

Secondly, we must ensure stringent control over the relationship between political parties and these industries. In an era when traditional media and journalists are often left high and dry, the temptation to use ready-made news from **PR** agencies is high. Moreover, with election campaigns becoming increasingly competitive and costly, politicians too can easily be lured by well-funded **PR** campaigns.

Representative democracy has weathered many storms in the past. I believe in its resilience to continue doing so, because the alternatives — chaos or dictatorship — are simply untenable.

Globalization vs democracy: A tangled affair

As we gallop into the twenty-first century, globalization sits in the driver's seat, turning the world into a mammoth stage for free trade and technological marvels. It has been the invisible hand, deftly remoulding our economic contours and subtly influencing societal norms like a proficient puppeteer. No wonder capitalism and consumer choice are frolicking gaily across the globe. But the catch here is, can we gift-wrap democracy and dispatch it worldwide just as easily?

The globalization bazaar seems to have developed quite a taste for democracy. It's also been a cradle for businesses with a knack for the "winner-takes-all" philosophy. High entry costs do an excellent job keeping competitors at bay once a behemoth like Facebook claims the lion's share of the market.

Take social media, for instance. They dangle the irresistible carrot of connecting with friends, all for free. But once they've charmed you into their realm and built a monopoly, the coin flips. Profits start flowing in through advertising and other means. Let's be clear: these are not naturally monopolistic businesses. Their fortress is made up of nothing but colossal capital reserves.

Now, this might seem like a jarring note in the sweet symphony of capitalism. But relax, it's merely a temporary hitch, not a death knell. It's just capitalism, growing pains and all.

Globalization's influence on democracy, however, is shrouded in a thicker mist. Anti-globalization squads are always ready with their placards decrying the loss of local power. But are they crusaders of democracy or covert advocates of a throwback to the darker times of authoritarianism or anarchism and communism?

Complicating the scene is the wave of immigration, often spurred on by dictatorships as welcoming as a thorn bush. Here's food for thought: should we vet asylum seekers and immigrants for their devotion to democracy, rather than their desire to flee conflict or poverty?

And then there's China, gorging on the banquet of globalization while coolly sidestepping international institutions and carving its own slice of the global economy. One might wonder if the Middle Kingdom should be coaxed into joining democratic clubs like the OECD.

With all its economic glitter, globalization can be a thorny path for democracy. Economic integration, border-fluidity, and the emergence of heavyweights like China pose gnarly questions for democratic institutions struggling to find their footing in this quaking landscape.

But let's not surrender democracy to the fright of globalization just yet. We must stand by the bastions of freedom, equality, and the rule of law. Let's not forget, they're the secret sauce to a fair society. Even in the face of swirling global currents, these ideals need to stand firm.

267

Democracy is no damsel in distress; it's a warrior, ready to take on the challenges of our ever-changing world.

268

11 The Limits of Representative Democracy

In the vast and bustling marketplace of political philosophies, representative democracy is a stall that has long been in the prime spot. It's championed as the solid stone bench upon which modern governance rests, yet this bench is not without its uncomfortable knots and splinters. In this chapter, we bravely prod and poke these discomforts, lifting the cosy blanket that often covers the less flattering crevices of representative democracy.

We set off by taking a hard look at the presumed marriage between "Democracy and Happiness". Does living under a democratic umbrella necessarily keep us dry from the drizzles of discontent? Or are we merely under a delusion of dryness while our feet are getting damp?

Our journey takes us next to the tricky terrain of "Too Much or Too Little Decentralization". Here, we ponder the Goldilocks problem of power distribution in a democracy - how much is just right to avoid local discontent, without stirring up national fragmentation?

Then, it's spotlight on "Lobby Regulation". We scrutinise this democratic backroom where policies are often massaged into shape, asking whether the current rules of engagement are up to the task of ensuring the masseurs don't have too firm a hand.

Our exploration veers towards the somewhat chillier territory of "Foreign Interference in Elections – Putin et al". We peel back the layers of the much-discussed allegations of foreign meddling, particularly by Russia, in what are supposed to be domestic democratic decisions.

Next, we turn our gaze towards "Free Media and Democracy", probing the role of the Fourth Estate in both nurturing and, perhaps at times, twisting the tree of democracy.

In "Social Media, Popular Delusions, and Democracy", we plunge into the digital rabbit hole, asking if these platforms help us up the democratic ladder or, just as easily, let us tumble down.

"The Danger of Rent-Seeking Behaviour" section pulls back the curtain on how democracies attempt to rein in those who seek to enrich themselves without adding societal value, thereby rocking the balance of resource distribution.

We then take a dive into "Democracy and Taxation", examining the public's sway over tax decisions, and whether this gives birth to equitable tax systems or merely feeds the ravenous beast of populism.

Lastly, we take a thoughtful sip from the chalice of "Democracy and Free Money", scrutinising ideas such as universal basic income, assessing their democratic taste and the implications for a society that links its notion of freedom with the availability of 'free' funds.

In this chapter, we embark on an unvarnished voyage through the less glamorous ports of representative democracy, not to downplay its triumphs, but to understand its trials. As we sail, we acknowledge that the ship of democracy, while sturdy, can cast long shadows that occasionally obscure the real challenges lying in its path. This isn't about throwing the ship's captain overboard; rather, it's about fine-tuning the vessel, so it's even better equipped for the journey ahead.

Democracy and happiness

It is difficult for humans to be happy on an empty stomach or without shelter. Yet, in most surveys about the sources of happiness, people usually rate higher other determinants of happiness such as family and health. So, it is wealth-creation (the main objective of capitalism) the only road to happiness? The answer is obviously no!

Different people pursue happiness in different ways, namely through meditation, friendship and many other ways that do not depend on the availability of the material comforts of life (see Layard, 2005). Yet, it is also unquestionable that the abundance of material comforts may facilitate or prevent the attainment of happiness.

One important factor to notice is that the pursuance of material wealth is often detrimental to the other factors contributing to human happiness, namely family life, community, and friends. However, most people will pursue wealth regardless of the economic system.

Therefore, as is often the case, the drive for wealth should not be confused with the results of an economic system (capitalist or other). For instance, imagine that humans were divided into two groups – satisfiers and maximizers. It will take a lot of reward to convince the first to emigrate and leave behind family and friends. So, in capitalism only its higher rewards can be blamed for enticing the urge to move on those individuals.

Nevertheless, the opposite is equally true. One should not ignore the key role played by wealth in family life. In particular the Portuguese adage that "in a hungry family all fight and none is right".

Indeed, the impact on family life and health through industrialization and urbanization was initially very disrupting and resented in the early days of capitalism, which led many social-minded philosophers to blame capitalism for that.

Likewise, long working hours, women employment and job insecurity often contribute to some of the greatest causes of unhappiness, namely separation/divorce and unemployment. Yet, this cannot be fairly attributed to capitalism, especially when we compare its working conditions with those under slavery, serfdom, or communism. Moreover, it gave women a degree of freedom never enjoyed in the past both in terms of self-supporting income and domestic help.

Of course, greater freedom inevitably comes

with a greater sense of insecurity. In particular, the freedom of contracting could not provide a job-for-life and the sense of security enjoyed by the serfs tied to the land. But, to some extent the state ended up replacing the landlords in providing unemployment insurance and other welfare programs. Moreover, it freed men from compulsory labor and military service which were a major cause of death.

Finally, at the cultural and moral levels, democracy and capitalism are often criticized as responsible for the loss of a sense of belonging and for growing resentment and envy, all factors that diminish happiness. Again, the greater freedom, wealth and opportunities created by democracy and capitalism in turn favored individualism, consumerism, and egalitarianism, which have happiness-reducing consequences. However, they also had significant happiness-increasing consequences in terms of liberty, abundance, and social mobility, which, on balance, are more important.

In conclusion, like all new systems, democracy and capitalism brought their own share of disruption to traditional values and certainties which wears down some sources of happiness. Although its facilitation of many other sources of happiness largely outweighs such erosion, there are some utopias that they cannot and should not promote, such as wealth equality. While equality of opportunity is indispensable for economic efficiency, trying to impose an equality of results would require eliminating individual risk and rewards and entrepreneurship which are fundamental for capitalism.

Too much or too little decentralization

Decentralization, in its many forms, is somewhat like cooking up a risotto. The dish, just like power, begins at a central point - the pot, or the central authority if you will. But then it gradually finds its way, much like the grain of rice, to regional or local governments. The intent? Empowering local communities and spicing up democratic participation. But there's a catch, or rather a Goldilocks problem.

It's a delicate dance to serve a risotto that is neither too dry nor too soupy. Similarly, with decentralization, tipping the scales too much could spark a bonfire of fragmentation and rebellion, throwing national unity into a hot pot. Too little, and you've got a recipe for exclusion and discontent simmering in local populations. The challenge? Stirring a balance where power is evenly spread, satisfying both the national palate and the local flavour.

Decentralization has long been the chef's

secret for enhancing political involvement and giving citizens a taste of ownership. Take a leaf out of the Federalist Papers, where it's noted that dishing out power makes for a robust representation of local needs. Sounds tasty, doesn't it? But let's not ignore the potential food poisoning here. The transfer of power can have some pretty unexpected side dishes.

Consider Spain and the United Kingdom, where giving too many cooks in the regional kitchen has resulted in some rather unpleasant dishes - separatist sentiments. Catalonia in Spain and Scotland in the UK are feeling a bit too chef-like for comfort, threatening the integrity of the nations. Here, our risotto suffers from too many flavours, creating a dish that's far from appealing at the national level.

Then you have Germany and Italy, the perfect risotto dishes. Born from the unification of several distinct flavours, or kingdoms, decentralization hasn't led to any bouts of food poisoning here. This goes to show that the results of decentralization depend heavily on the recipe used.

Throw in a mix of religious or ethnic ingredients, like in the India and Pakistan partition, and you have a potential kitchen disaster. Therefore, it's critical to check the freshness and compatibility of your ingredients - the ethnic and religious fabric - before deciding on your cooking method.

Spain, while mastering the art of cooking at home, is also participating in a multinational MasterChef called the European Union. The EU, with its advocacy for regional autonomy and integration, has raised the temperature in Spain's kitchen, where there's already smoke from too much decentralization.

As such, while decentralization may promise a gourmet meal of participatory governance, it needs the right recipe - subsidiarity. It's not a ready-made meal solution. A slow-cooking method, like gradual deconcentrating of services, could be the secret to a perfectly cooked decentralization risotto.

In conclusion, the question of too much or too little decentralization is the ultimate culinary challenge. It calls for a master chef's understanding of the social and political ingredients at hand, a respect for their historical taste profiles, and a clever balance of local, national, and global flavours. By carefully adjusting the heat and stirring rhythm of decentralization, it's possible to serve a democratic feast that satisfies all, without leaving a bitter taste of national disunity.

Lobby regulation

Lobbying, in the democratic dinner party, is like a sneaky piece of spicy gossip that circulates among the guests, secretly swaying their opinions. It is a dance between interest groups and policymakers, with an ultimate goal to influence the decision-making choreography. The freedom to associate and express allows for these special interest groups to form, a bit like canapés gathering on a platter. Some countries, like the United States, acknowledge this party chit-chat and even regulate it. In others, it remains hushed whispers behind the scenes.

Lobbyists, our culinary multi-taskers, add a variety of flavours to this political feast. They fund campaigns like a generous sprinkling of truffles, engage in public affairs, and shape policies. This democratic kitchen is where policies often rise like soufflés, and it's worth donning an apron to scrutinise the process. The current recipes need a review to ensure these policy chefs are not adding an overpowering amount of their own flavour.

Regulating lobbying is much like distinguishing between the generous sharing of a recipe and stealing it outright. The "ComEd 4" trial in the US, where the accused were found guilty of bribing to influence, is a stark reminder of this. Like a spoiled dish at a banquet, it underscores the need for a sharper knife in the regulation of lobbying activities.

The scene changes in countries where lobbying, like an exotic ingredient, lacks official recognition and regulation. Take Portugal, where top law firms bag substantial revenues from government contracts, largely unregulated. This buffet-style approach offers a smorgasbord of opportunities for corruption and highlights the importance of a well-written menu of lobbying regulation.

Internationally, there's been some progress in cooking up rules for lobbying. The OECD, our global kitchen supervisor, rolled out the Recommendation on Principles for Transparency and Integrity in Lobbying in 2010. This unique recipe aims to prevent lobbying from spoiling the democratic broth. A growing number of nations are agreeing on the need for clear labelling (transparency), and fourteen OECD members have adopted lobbying regulations. However, many of these rules seem more like hastily prepared dishes to quell a scandal rather than thoughtfully planned meals, putting their cost-effectiveness into question.

Clearly, lobbying regulation needs more time

in the oven. We must ensure transparency and accountability in the operations of interest groups, just as a good chef is accountable for their kitchen. An effective lobbying rulebook should promote open access to lawmakers, mandatory disclosure of lobbying activities, and strict sanctions for rule breaking.

To sum up, just as a good spread is integral to a dinner party, the freedom to associate is fundamental to democracy and lobbying. Yet, unchecked, and unregulated lobbying can turn a democratic feast into a free-for-all buffet. As such, we need robust, future-proof lobbying rules that ensure the integrity of the democratic process, maintain transparency, and prevent undue influence and corruption. After all, in this democratic kitchen, we're all responsible for the meal we end up with.

Foreign interference in elections – Putin et al

The scandal swirling around Putin's supposed dabbling in the US elections to hoist Trump into the White House is as intriguing as it is unsettling. It's rather like rummaging in a bag of mixed nuts - a handful could contain anything from the benignly crunchy to the unsavoury hard shells. It's a question of deciding between plain old networking between politically aligned parties, and the decidedly murkier territory of states dispatching their secret services to meddle in foreign elections.

Picture this: Putin, or one of his comrades, strutting onto the stage at a Republican rally, warmly embraced by Trump. Now, in the world's truly democratic quarters, this isn't a sight that would cause much of a stir. It's nothing more than political pageantry, much like Merkel cosying up to the Spanish Popular Party, or Felipe Gonzalez shaking hands with the Portuguese Socialists. These public displays are simply part and parcel of politics.

The muddier waters are when this camaraderie takes on a different guise - financial donations, technical aid, or extra hands-on deck, all funnelled in through the backdoor. Here, the question becomes one of legality and financial accountability. If these transactions are properly accounted for and meet legal standards, then it's all above board, provided any quid pro quo is also out in the open. But it's not always as simple as exchanging campaign support for a friendly policy stance. Sometimes, it involves a more insidious trading of political and business favours, where the transparency crucial to democracy starts to cloud over.

The darker the shadows that shroud this support, the greater the threat to democracy. It's a particularly thorny issue when these transactions are carried out by intermediaries not directly affiliated with states or parties. But don't be too quick to label all these interventions as anti-democratic. For instance, Germany's intricate network of business-backed foundations and trade associations offer a more nuanced perspective. These organisations cover the full gamut of political leanings and, while subtly bolstered by the state, their main aim is to quietly champion German investments and exports. So perhaps, the game of international politics is not all that black and white, but rather an intricate mosaic of greys.

Turning our attention to the less palatable side of political financing, we stumble upon the scenario of Marie Le Pen cosying up to a Putin-affiliated bank for a loan. It's a rather like turning up to a high-brow dinner party with a discount supermarket wine - it might do the job, but it's unlikely to win you any admirers. Yes, it's perfectly acceptable for political factions to pass around the begging bowl to national banks, but the waters start to muddy when foreign affiliations come into play.

In our grand political theatre, there's another act that truly steals the spotlight in terms of its scandalous overtones: unsolicited support. This is like an uninvited guest crashing your meticulously planned soiree. It's these spontaneous, non-consensual contributions that can pack a real punch in the political landscape, and not in a good way.

Free media and democracy

As a wee lad, my weekends were punctuated by the flickering lights of the cinema screen. As heartwarming as the nostalgic sepia-tones of Cinema Paradiso, this scene played out not just in Portugal, but across Europe, which was enjoying its heyday in film during the 1940s.

However, every sunset has its dawn. As televisions began popping up in living rooms, cinema took a nosedive. It's akin to having your favourite restaurant replaced by a newfangled food delivery service. The winds of change blow, and suddenly we're left wondering why movie-making meccas sprouted in some regions, like Hollywood and Bollywood, while Europe's film garden wilted.

Historian Tony Judt shed some light on this in his tome, 'Postwar'. He pointed a rather accusatory finger at the US State Department, suggesting it used Hollywood films as Trojan horses, flooding European markets to garner anti-Communist sentiments.

Europe, not to be outdone, struck back, with governments from across the political spectrum rallying to save their faltering film industries. Quotas were enforced, subsidies were doled out. However, in the face of this technological tidal wave, their efforts were akin to bringing a knife to a gunfight. They mistook innovation for competition and ended up hobbling the very industries they sought to save.

To add insult to injury, the 60s witnessed these well-intentioned but ultimately misplaced policies birthing a subsidised cottage industry. In walked the Left-leaning intellectual crowd, a parade of directors, from Truffaut to Godard, who would eventually go on to hobnob at the Cannes Film Festival.

Now, let's be clear. With the prevalence of DVDs and a recent boom in multiplexes, cinema-going isn't completely extinct. But producing films for domestic consumption just doesn't have the financial appeal it once did. The Portuguese film industry, for example, is in a pickle. Their most successful domestic film raked in a measly 300,000 Euros, barely covering half the cost of a budget production. Not exactly a gold mine, unless you're a political-minded 'intellectual' with an artistic itch to scratch.

Now, with the Internet huffing and puffing at the doors of traditional broadcast television, we're in for another round of industry shake-up. Could the likes of YouTube be the next big bogeyman for television and film producers? And how should Europe respond this time? I would gently suggest that perhaps, instead of fortifying their walls against foreign invasion, they might consider learning from past follies.

Otherwise, we might see yet another 'Cinema Paradiso' play out, with Europe reduced to a bit of a player in the theatre of creative industries. Worst still, it will seriously damage the democratic prospects.

Social media, popular delusions, and democracy

In the merry month of May 2012, Facebook was ceremoniously flung onto the public market, causing an absolute storm. Shares flew off the metaphorical shelf, eventually settling at a number so dazzlingly high it would've given a mathematician a headache. And at the eye of this tempest stood a young, slightly awkward chap called Mark Zuckerberg, Facebook's inventor, now cradling a wealth that could make Midas blanch.

Facebook, the digital home to every seventh person on this spinning globe, was being valued at a whopping 26 times its sales. For a moment, let's play the role of Doubting Thomases. Could Facebook, however beloved it might be, rake in profits hefty enough to justify such a mind-boggling figure? Odds are, probably not.

It's tradition at this point for economic seers to step onto their soapboxes, decrying the rampant irrationality plaguing the markets, the speculative madness that tumbles into the abyss of Ponzi-esque schemes. They wag their fingers, cautioning us that this may be yet another sign of capitalism's decay, the harbinger of the need for a system overhaul.

But history is a crafty old woman with a bag full of tales. She tells us of tulips, canals, railways, dot.com companies - each has had its moment basking in the intoxicating sunlight of mania, only to retire under the shade of sober reality. These episodes, volatile as they may be, serve as release valves for societal frustrations that intermittently bubble up.

Here's the twist in the tale, though. Social media platforms like Facebook, which have arguably turned the world into a noisy global neighbourhood, can also perpetuate mass delusions at a scale we've never witnessed before. The chirping bird of Twitter, under the wing of the notoriously unpredictable Elon Musk, has already started leaning towards a pro-Putin tilt. Is it Musk's personal bent or Russian roubles lining his pockets? Only time will reveal the truth. But it serves as a chilling reminder of the power social media wields over our democracies.

So, what's the solution? Simple but not easy: we need to keep our heads about us. Social media platforms, though revolutionary, must be used judiciously, both by those who concoct them in Silicon Valley labs and those of us who populate them. Perhaps a dash of policy intervention wouldn't go amiss to curb misinformation and uphold the integrity of our democratic processes.

Yet at the end of the day, while we should continue to prod and question, let's not throw the baby out with the bathwater. As we navigate the idiosyncrasies of capitalism, let's remember: Be prudent, but don't blame the system.

The danger of rent-seeking behaviour

Business regulation, once deeply entangled in the thickets of antitrust policies and barriers to entry, now finds itself tussling with a different creature altogether: rent-seeking behaviour. No longer confined to government-sanctioned monopolies or oligopolies, rent-seeking behaviour has spread its wings. It's about squirrelling profits, not by creating new wealth but by sneakily manoeuvring the socio-political machinery that churns our economy. It's a game often played to the detriment of others and, by extension, society at large.

Imagine industries such as healthcare, taxi services, pharmaceuticals, or natural monopolies like landownership as magnets for rent-seeking. In these arenas, however, sectors dominated by a single player can show similar traits. In industries that welcome newcomers with open arms, innovators might relish a temporary monopoly. But give it some time, and their monopoly crumbles to dust, swept away by the horde of copycats nibbling away at profits until there are no "rents" to speak of.

Now, let's change the scene a bit to sectors governed by a "winner-takes-all" dynamic. The competition here is more like a high-stakes lottery where it carries on until one player secures market dominance. The victors, beaming with their jackpot, often either retreat into a cosy retirement or transform into private equity predators, gobbling up any emerging innovators threatening their throne. This survival-of-the-fittest scenario isn't inherently bad - many "serial entrepreneurs" relish finding new business opportunities and jump at the chance to cash-in rapidly.

But the plot thickens when these dominant players flex their financial muscles to hamstring the natural selection of winners. Facebook's eye-watering $20 billion acquisition of Instagram and WhatsApp is a case in point. Was this mammoth move a strategic play to fortify Facebook's stronghold in global photo-sharing and mobile messaging, or did the giant stomp on the competition process prematurely?

In the traditional media landscape, do we wring our hands over Rupert Murdoch's reins over several right-leaning newspapers and TV channels? Maybe not, as long as there's room for other players - think Ted Turner - with different political inclinations to join the game.

But a real head-scratcher arises in the "winner-takes-all" sectors where we have to step in to shield democracy from the potential fallouts of market dominance. Walking the tightrope between market regulation and unnecessary meddling is a delicate balancing act. Take the financial sector, for example, where regulatory overkill often ends up shielding the big guns who can weather the storm of stringent rules.

To sum up, while regulation plays a critical role in thwarting rent-seeking behaviour and industry monopolisation, we must ensure it doesn't choke competition or innovation. In arenas where the ideal level of regulation is a bit of a mystery, it's wise to tip the scale towards under-regulation, promoting robust market competition and innovation. The role of regulators then becomes crucial in ensuring fair play and preventing any player from becoming so omnipotent that they can twist the rules to suit their whims. In doing so, we can nurture an ecosystem that sparks democratic and entrepreneurial spirit while fending off rent-seeking tendencies.

Democracy, liberalism, and taxation

Recall the old war cry, "no taxation without representation"? It seems quaint now, doesn't it? But let's unpack that. You see, contrary to popular belief, constitutional liberalism doesn't just require the state to act as a bodyguard or a referee. The state isn't merely expected to provide policing, defense, and justice, or act as a neutral arbiter. Rather, it's meant to be a custodian, acting solely in a supporting role and keeping its fingers off too many pies, especially those of wealth redistribution.

Libertarians and classical liberals usually argue that the state should stick to funding the basics - defense, police, justice - using taxes, preferably a flat tax. They tend to view progressive taxes, not to mention inheritance taxes, as an affront, an inefficient reshuffling of wealth that penalises the hard grafters among us.

But, unlike its laissez-faire cousin, constitutional liberalism has fewer qualms about inheritance taxes and a progressive tax system. In fact, it may view both as crucial to prevent the wealthy from hitching a free ride and to keep market capitalism alive. Let me explain.

Consider government services as insurance coverage. Every good libertarian will agree that the state should protect us and our property from predators, foreign and domestic. Paying taxes for that protection is much like paying an insurance premium. A flat tax rate might seem fair because it appears to be proportionate to the capital at risk. But here's the rub - just as an insurance company takes risk into account when calculating premiums, the state should tax those who add more risk to the community. Since greater wealth attracts more predators and adds more collective risk, it only follows that the wealthy should pay more.

But why should the rich pay to alleviate poverty? Because poverty breeds crime, and it is in the interest of the wealthy to prevent crime (much like they pay for private security). Thus, even without any philanthropic motives, the rich should pay more taxes to alleviate poverty - taxation must be progressive.

The argument for inheritance taxes is a tad more complicated. These taxes curb wealth accumulation, which might seem counterproductive, given that saving and accumulation promote growth. There's a case for limiting corporate wealth to prevent oligopolies and ensure market competition, but the argument for limiting private wealth isn't as straightforward.

Consider the role of credit in a capitalist system and the availability of near-risk-free investment opportunities in government debt financing. If left unchecked, over time, debt financing and the magic of compound interest would result in a single entity owning all the world's wealth. Unthinkable? Let's play a game. Let's say you are part of a long-standing institution, say a religious congregation. Now, estimate the interest rate required for your institution to accumulate all the world's wealth.

As an example, let's consider the priests at the Temple of Jerusalem who paid Judas thirty pieces of silver (around $15,000 today) for his betrayal of Jesus. If they'd invested that sum in risk-free debt at an interest rate of 1.28% per year, they'd now own the world's wealth, estimated at almost $2,000 trillion.

Of course, the scenario is more complex if multiple institutions attempt the same approach. They'd probably be at each other's throats after a millennium or so. The Catholic Church, for instance, never came close to owning all the world's wealth, thanks to periodic expropriation by various rulers and risky investments in relics and art.

However, a 20% inheritance tax every fifty years would considerably slow down the accumulation of wealth. It wouldn't eliminate wealth concentration, but it certainly curbs it, without resorting to war and confiscation.

I've made my case assuming tax neutrality, but one could argue that taxation as a social and economic tool fits comfortably within constitutional liberalism and representative democracy. Regardless, debates about the tax pie's size and the practicalities of tax collection are crucial. As the saying goes, "The art of taxation consists in so plucking the goose as to obtain the largest possible number of feathers with the smallest possible amount of hissing." And that, my friends, is a delicate art indeed.

Democracy and free money

The seemingly utopian notion of 'free money,' particularly championed in the guise of Universal Basic Income (UBI) and Universal Social Inheritance (USI), has been a bee in the bonnet of social reformers in recent years. It's hailed as a magic wand to wave away poverty and income inequality. Yet, its democratic implications and effects on societies that equate liberty with an abundance of 'free' funds need a fine-toothed comb run through them. Although free money's charm is palpable, it's a Pandora's box of possible pitfalls, stirring up sloth, spawning wastefulness, and opening the floodgates for corruption.

Let's not kid ourselves: imagining our government as a mere Robin Hood, stealing from the rich to give to the poor, is a dangerous oversimplification. It's a dangerously naive view that glosses over the knotty webs of social and economic intricacies and underestimates the boomerang effect of adverse consequences, including injustices, the free-riding, and the wormhole of corruption.

Consider Venezuela, where the despotic regime manages to cling to power partly by playing Santa Claus and distributing government handouts. Trapped in the grip of poverty, a significant segment of the population has become hooked on these handouts, inadvertently buttressing a repressive system that stifles their freedom and potential.

Indeed, even in democratic bastions, an overdose of free money can skew the political and economic seesaw. Portugal makes for an interesting case study. Despite decades of economic stagnation, the Socialist party remains firmly ensconced in power, thanks largely to a sprawling web of subsidies that covers almost two-thirds of the populace. Toss in the fact that half of Portugal's denizens are exempt from income tax and the European Union's munificent funds, and you get a cocktail of unproductive government spending. Such generosity makes voters turn a blind eye to the government's spendthrift ways.

The problem of free money isn't confined to national borders, though. It rears its head in the international arena too, notably in the form of foreign aid. Despite its noble intentions of poverty alleviation and sparking growth in less developed countries, a pitifully small portion of the aid provided ever reaches its intended beneficiaries. The lion's share is often drained away due to inefficiencies, corruption, and mismanagement.

So, the penny drops. While doling out free money may serve as a temporary plaster and secure fleeting political wins, it potentially gnaws at the foundations of democratic values, economic resilience, and societal responsibility.

Rather than nursing a culture of handout dependency, democratic governments should roll up their sleeves and focus on nurturing conditions that spur economic growth and self-sustainability. Education, training programmes, and similar initiatives can help people help themselves, stimulate productivity, and rev up the economic engine. Instead of handing out free money willy-nilly, governments should invest in public services and infrastructure, thereby cultivating a business-friendly environment that seeds job creation.

In the same vein, international aid should be

put under the microscope and tied to specific projects or goals to ensure funds reach the people they're meant to benefit. Let's focus on bolstering local capacities and nurturing self-sustainability, not breeding dependency.

In a nutshell, 'free money,' be it in the form of UBI/USI, subsidies, or foreign aid, may seem a tantalising prospect, especially in democracies where political power can be wooed or retained by pandering to immediate needs. However, the long game paints a sobering picture: dependency, complacency, corruption. A true democracy and real freedom demand a citizenry that's responsible, values the dignity of labour, and champions sustainable economic growth.

12 The Future of Democracy

If there's anything about democracy that baffles me more than the Brexit debacle or the 2016 US presidential election, it's that for all its obvious, aching flaws, we've yet to come up with anything better. Flick on the telly or trawl through Twitter, and you'll discover both the glory and the folly of a system that leaves the fate of a nation in the hands of its people.

And yet, in this chapter, we'll consider if the many futures we've imagined — from Star Trek's utopian Federation to Orwell's grimly totalitarian Oceania — might hold some hint as to the path we'll eventually tread. It seems science fiction views of democracy provide more than just popcorn-fuelled entertainment.

Then, we'll turn our attention to the wearying nature of democracy itself. If you've ever felt the urge to roll your eyes at the arrival of another polling card, or a sinking sense of dread at the prospect of a political debate on TV, you're not alone. Democracy, in its relentless pursuit of fairness, can be an exhausting affair, akin to arguing with a persistent but well-meaning in-law at a family gathering. Is there any wonder some of us yearn for a break?

Moving on, we'll tackle the slippery eel that is globalization. In an increasingly interconnected world, our democratic systems have had to grapple with forces that refuse to recognize the boundaries of nations or the quaint notion of sovereign control. The question is, can our democracy adapt to these global pressures, or will it crumble like a poorly made biscuit under the weight of its own tea?

From here, we'll take a detour to consider if democracy can outlive capitalism. Surely a system that is inherently fair but tends to concentrate wealth in the hands of the few can't peacefully coexist with one that values the voice of the many? Yet here we are, with Wall Street and Washington in a seemingly eternal dance. Can this duet continue into the future or will the music eventually stop?

Next, we must consider the impact of information technology and representation. Here, democracy finds itself at an odd crossroads. On one side, a brave new world of direct, digitized representation; on the other, the disquieting possibility of an AI future that makes our collective human voice obsolete. Do we welcome our robot overlords or rally for a techno-peasant revolt?

Speaking of futures, we'll also venture into the notion of democracy without representation. It sounds like a mad idea, like trying to make a souffle without eggs, but there are those who believe it possible. We'll explore this counter-intuitive idea, and wonder if it holds any water or if it's simply a leaky bucket.

Finally, we'll end with a look at ageing and democracy. As we extend our life expectancy, do we likewise extend the vitality of our democracy, or do we risk becoming a nation of doddering fools, unable to decide between the lesser of two evils?

From the fantastical to the mundane, from technology's rapid progress to the steady march of time, democracy is at a crossroads. Where we go from here is uncertain, but let's take a journey together through the looking glass and see if we can glimpse our collective democratic destiny.

Science fiction views of democracy

There's something deliciously diverse about science fiction's take on politics. It's like a pick 'n' mix of the good, the bad, and the simply bonkers – a sort of political rummage sale, if you will. From anarchy to totalitarianism, the genre's musings span the full spectrum of governance, serving up a smorgasbord of possibilities for our future selves.

Consider H.G. Wells' 'The Time Machine', a cautionary tale of social Darwinism on steroids, with humanity evolving into entirely different species based on social class. It's an extreme view, yes, but one that plays beautifully into our fears of what might happen if we let our class divisions run rampant.

The genre can do utopias too, mind you. Take Thomas More's 'Utopia' for instance. But don't be fooled. In science fiction, the utopia is often less about the idyllic society itself and more about the fun and games its inhabitants have navigating the system. We see this in the epic 'Star Wars' saga where convoluted interstellar politics rule the day and historical events seem to have a knack for repeating themselves.

A bit more cloak and dagger are the tales of conspiracy and paranoia, where secret forces lurk in the shadows, plotting the heroes' downfall. Anyone read the 'Illuminatus! Trilogy'? You'll get the gist.

Philip K. Dick's 'The Minority Report' presents another interesting wrinkle. Imagine, if you will, a world where crimes can be foreseen with such precision that they can be stopped before they occur. It's not just the tech that's interesting here, it's the can of legal and political worms it flings wide open.

L. Neil Smith's libertarian science fiction, kicking off with 'The Probability Broach', paints a picture of an alternate United States, one that took a sharp left turn away from centralized power after its birth. Food for thought, isn't it?

And then there's Robert A. Heinlein's 'Starship Troopers' where democracy is a privilege to be earned through service. A daring proposition that stirs up the age-old debate on who should get a say in governance.

More recently, 'Black Mirror' series broaches the effects of unchecked tech growth on democracy. It's a chilling reminder of the dangers lurking in our digital age, where social media can sway the masses and disrupt the democratic process.

So, as we delve into the world of science fiction, we're not just adding to an already hefty pile of scenarios. We're reassessing current trends, dissecting what they could mean for our future, and perhaps looking for ways to steer our course wisely. After all, isn't that what good fiction is all about?

About the tiring nature of democracy

Democracy, hailed as the zenith of political evolution, seems to be running a marathon in a world primed for a sprint. It's a robust beast, built to include every voice in the chorus of governance, but it also seems to have a bad case of political lumbago. It's not the machinery of democracy that's weary; it's the complex social, political, and psychological tapestry it weaves that leaves us rubbing our temples.

Imagine democracy as a grand, cumbersome, antique clock, demanding time for discussion, debate, and the meticulous shaping of policies. In a world that's forever on the fast-forward button, the deliberative ballet of democracy can feel like watching paint dry. The consensus-seeking, the checking, the balancing, the scrutiny - they are democracy's lifeblood, but they also have a knack for applying brakes on swift decision-making.

Adding to this democratic malaise is a growing mistrust in the democratic process itself. It's as if democracy has put its hearing aid on mute, amplifying only a select few voices and leaving the rest in the soundless void. The political glitterati, cut from the same cloth, appear increasingly alienated from the everyday realities of the hoi polloi. This sense of disconnect is like a slow leak, gradually deflating public faith in the system.

Political life, once a noble crusade akin to public service, now seems like a treadmill for career politicians. Our representatives appear to be more obsessed with their hold on power than serving the public, widening the chasm between the rulers and the ruled.

There are whispers of offloading political activity to a select elite or even machines. Yet, such proposals threaten to gut democracy of its essence - power to the people. Proxies, even under the banner of general commands, can't capture the throbbing diversity and dynamism inherent in a democratic populace.

However, democracy, as resilient as an old soldier, fights on. Echoing Winston Churchill's gruff wisdom, democracy might be the worst form of government, except for everything else we've tried. While democracy may be a bit of a slog, it still beats the competition. Its saving grace is its capacity to correct itself, to adapt, and to respond to the needs of its people.

The way forward involves pumping some fresh blood into our democratic systems. We need to cultivate a more varied political landscape, find shortcuts in decision-making without sacrificing rigour, and harness technology to make political participation less of a chore.

In conclusion, democracy might be a tiring slog, but its undying commitment to freedom, equality, and people's voice make it worth the struggle for another 500 years.

Democracy and globalization

Will democracy sweep across the globe like contagion? Perhaps. But is a world united under a single political banner something to cheer for? Not quite, because a dash of variety in political systems adds flavour to the global potpourri. The real question, however, is whether the twin forces of democracy and globalization can waltz together without treading on each other's toes.

The naysayers of globalization sling mud at it from three angles: it's the cultural Grim Reaper, it's a field day for multinationals looking to exploit lax regulations and non-unionized labour in poorer countries, and it's an insidious worm eating away at national sovereignty.

But let's look at the flip side. Globalization, hand-in-hand with capitalism, is like a global broom sweeping away extreme poverty. The ripple effect touches health, education, consumption - the fundamentals of human life.

The real impact, though, lies in how globalization shakes up political structures and regulatory systems. It's a double-edged sword, simultaneously bolstering and undermining the need for regulation. For instance, as goods, labour, and capital trot freely around the globe, the reins of national governments slacken. But the prospect of sudden, large-scale movements, which could send tremors through infrastructure and employment, underlines the need for global regulation.

Let's dip our toes into some hypotheticals. Could we have an international court presiding over violations of the rule of law? And if so, would it lean on common law or civil law? These questions pull us into the labyrinthine debate on how to construct a multilayered government structure - from local to global - within a democratic framework.

Though we are slowly spinning the thread of internationally accepted laws, weaving a comprehensive legal tapestry might take centuries. Perhaps, the fastest route would be through a step-by-step integration at the regional level, much like the European Union.

In conclusion, while democracy and globalization are star-crossed lovers, pushing one to run before it can walk could trip them both up. It's a delicate dance, and we must ensure that the rhythm of one doesn't trip the other.

Will democracy outlive capitalism?

Pondering whether democracy will outlive capitalism is like wondering if an old married couple will celebrate their golden anniversary. They were born separately, yes – democracy being the ancient Athenian and capitalism the upstart from the Renaissance – but it's been so long since their union that it's hard to imagine them parting ways.

Now, it's worth noting that capitalism, with its powerful lifecycle, is like the charismatic partner who has a penchant for reinventing themselves. It's likely that capitalism, in its current form, will exit stage left, to be replaced by an upgraded version. Picture it – an old, greying capitalist model trotting off to make way for a new, sparkling, silicon-enhanced counterpart.

But let's not get ahead of ourselves. This metamorphosis won't be an overnight affair. We'd see the same old capitalism continuing to churn out wealth while its time-honored principles quietly fade into the background, to be replaced by the shiny, digital rules of the new era. If we were to label this future epoch, I'd cheekily suggest calling it the "Robo-Capitalism Age" – the age of material contentment and ubiquitous mechanical laborers.

Reaching this fantastical age requires a bit of a wealth shuffle, mind you. We'd need to see some capital spread around via inheritance or wealth taxes; else we might end up with a society more elitist than a private members' club in Mayfair. The peasants with pitchforks scenario aren't quite as appealing.

Alternatively, we could spread the wealth around through shared and state property. Imagine humanoid robots and the non-personal stock of capital becoming community property. Sounds dreamy, but it might leave our new economic system a bit limp, like a cocktail party without cocktails.

Regardless of the route we choose, it's pretty clear that the profit motive, the beating heart of capitalism, might take a hit in this new age. We'd swap the greed and grubbiness of profits for the cold, calculated efficiency of profit-maximizing robots. Imagine machines obediently following our economic orders, like a well-trained spaniel fetching a ball.

And what about democracy? Well, in this robo-capitalist utopia, politics might find itself as the last bastion of human activity. We'd have more plebiscite democracy than you could shake a ballot paper at. Alternatively, we could delegate our democratic duties to AI, making politics as personalized as ordering a custom sandwich at your local deli.

It's an appealing vision — capitalism and democracy evolving together like the old couple who, despite their idiosyncrasies, continue to walk hand in hand. But it's just a vision, after all. Whether reality will follow this charming script, only time will tell.

Information technology and representation

As we wade deeper into the digital quagmire, information technology and political representation are starting to look more like partners in crime than odd bedfellows. They've both pulled up a chair at the table, swapping notes over a cocktail of social media, data analytics, and artificial intelligence. It's a powerful brew that's tinkering with the way we interact with our democratic institutions and the people who represent us. The result? We're staring down the barrel of some major shake-ups to our electoral systems, democratic practices, and the quality of our representation.

On the shiny side of the coin, information technology is throwing open the gates to new, sophisticated voting systems. Think of it as the tech-world's own political revolution, changing the way we count votes and run election campaigns. The real poster child here is candidate weighting - a method that lets voters rank their preferences. Like a powerful filter, it distils the will of the majority and sidesteps divisive electoral outcomes. But this isn't an 'install and play' kind of system - it needs some serious tech support for smooth sailing.

But let's not start popping the champagne just yet. Technology's track record in politics has had a few hits and misses. Cue the ghost of scandals past, like the infamous Cambridge Analytica. Instead of playing the honest informer, they played puppeteer, using information technology to pull the strings of voter behavior. A sobering reminder that the power of technology is as sharp and double-edged as a surgeon's scalpel.

It's undeniable that information technology is crammed with potential to bolster or bash democratic representation. It's a virtual goldmine of opportunities to shed light on the murky election process and boost transparency. Imagine having the power to fact-check political promises in real-time or unearth hidden agendas behind policy decisions. If used properly, these tools could play the lead role in a political version of "Illumination", helping to create a more informed electorate and accountable representatives.

Then again, information technology is stoking the fires of debate about alternative forms of democracy, like plebiscite democracy. This is the VIP club of democracy, where the public gets to vote directly on specific issues, skipping the need for representatives. It's an attractive proposition, but it comes with its own baggage, like the risk of uninformed voting or the tyranny of the majority.

Ultimately, the impact of information technology on representation will hinge on our handling of it. As they say, technology is a tool. The way we wield it, guided by democratic principles and ethical codes, will decide whether it's a tonic or toxin for representation. Used with care, it could be the adrenaline shot that supercharges the democratic process. Mishandled, it can twist public discourse, manipulate voters, and drain trust in the democratic process.

To sum it up, information technology is no longer knocking at the door of the political landscape - it's already inside, rearranging the furniture. Its potential to tweak voting systems, expose hidden interests, and spark alternative forms of democracy is staggering. But it's not without its challenges - manipulation risks and potential erosion of representative democracy are hard pills to swallow. As we tread this digital tightrope, we must be vigilant, guided by firm ethical standards and robust legal frameworks.

Our mission? To harness technology not as a weapon of distortion and manipulation, but as a beacon to enlighten and empower.

Democracy without representation?

"Democracy without representation?" you ask. This question is a bit like asking "Can I have a cake without flour?" You can try, but the end result is going to be rather disappointing.

First, we have the obvious substitutes like direct democracy and plebiscite democracy, sort of like using almond flour or gluten-free mix for your cake. It might seem appealing at first, especially for those allergic to gluten (or, in our analogy, allergic to politicians). However, they often result in a far less palatable dish (or a society teetering dangerously close to mob rule).

Imagine using a lottery system to elect our officials. That's a bit like expecting your cat to bake the cake for you. Sure, cats are smart and they can pull off some surprising feats, but would you really trust Whiskers with your Victoria sponge?

Then there's the rotation roster, the equivalent of letting each of your children take turns making the cake. Once upon a time, I was a Dean of a Faculty with this system in place. We ended up with some interesting creations, not all of them edible. When we switched to proper elections, the results weren't much better, and our "kitchen" became a political battleground. Turns out, kids (or in our case, faculty members) don't like sharing the fun job of cake-making (or the power that comes with being Dean).

Let's not forget the idea of randomly picking our representatives, which is as risky as closing your eyes, opening a cookbook, and pointing to a recipe. Sure, there's a chance you'll pick a delicious dessert, but there's also a good chance you'll end up trying to serve roast beef for dessert.

In the end, these alternatives to representative democracy are like trying to replace flour in a cake recipe. You might end up with something vaguely resembling a cake, but it won't quite hit the spot. You see, in a representative democracy, we're not just voting for a person, but an ideology, a direction, a way to move forward. And that's what makes it the essential ingredient in the recipe for a thriving democracy.

So, as you can see, democracy without representation is like cake without flour - you could try, but it's likely to be a half-baked idea.

Ageing and democracy

The grey hairs are growing, and there are more than just a few sprinkled about. The democratic geriatrics club is having a field day, basking in the glory of medical breakthroughs and improved standards of living. What's the downside, you ask? Well, we're skating on thin democratic ice, friends. The age balance in our societies is wobbling like an unsteady grandparent without their walking stick.

Democracy - let's boil it down to its essence - is everyone getting their fair say. The granny and grandpa brigade, however, seem to be holding the microphone just a tad too long. It's like a family dinner where the elders dominate the conversation, and the young ones are barely getting a word in edgeways. If we aren't careful, we're looking at an all-out generational arm-wrestling match with fairness, equity, and representation on the line.

The oldies, they've been around the block a few times and they've seen it all. They get tired, disillusioned even. The younglings, bless their hearts, are often too busy Snapchatting to care. To add to the mix, 'adulting' seems to be a thing of the late thirties rather than early twenties these days. Everyone seems to be clinging to their parent's apron strings just a bit longer.

But before we panic, let's be clear: we're not suggesting putting a lid on the older generation's votes. That's an affront to democracy. The challenge is to ensure the youngsters aren't left out in the cold. It's a Herculean task, of course. But what we need to do is pave the way for better cross-generational chit-chat, develop a political landscape that doesn't put the young or the old in the shade.

To light the way, why not coax more of the young 'uns into the political fold? Maybe tweak civic education to catch their interest, drop the voting age a notch or two, or heck, let's get trendy with some digital voting methods. Legislation should also keep an ear out for what gets the youth fired up - be it climate change, affordable education, or job opportunities.

What's more, we need to move beyond a tug-of-war between generations. It's high time we appreciated the beauty of different age cohorts coming together to weave a more robust social fabric. Let's put the 'us vs. them' narrative on the shelf and set up platforms where the young, the old, and those in between can jointly mold our policies.

Sure, we're riding the demographic wave and there's no turning back. But it's far from a doomsday scenario for democracy. It calls for a bit of creativity, flexibility, and a good dose of grit. We've got to keep our democratic spirit alive, and navigate the tides, ensuring that our societal ship doesn't sink.

Because, let's face it, democracy isn't just about governance. It's a pact we make - an agreement to look out for everyone's rights and interests, whether they're just starting out in life or have a lifetime of experiences under their belt. Our aging societies should not only be a source of pride, but also a catalyst for reinforcing our democratic spirit.

In a nutshell, the more candles we add to our societal birthday cake, the more we realize the democratic tune we're playing. The melody's got to keep going, and every note - whether it's delivered in a youthful pitch or a matured tone - deserves to ring out loud and clear. Let's keep the music playing, folks, with each and every voice contributing to our shared symphony of democratic governance.

About the Six Pillars for the Good of Humanity

In life, where the drama of history plays out with us as both audience and actors, I found myself pondering a question that has likely tickled the grey cells of many before me: what legacy do I leave for those who follow? The usual suspects crossed my mind – tales of love, the bonds of family, the camaraderie of friends, and the trials and tribulations of upbringing. But, having had the mixed fortune of growing up under the stern gaze of Salazar and his rather austere corporatist regime, only to blossom in the more freewheeling world of democratic regimes and capitalist systems, my musings took a more structural turn.

You see, these regimes, for all their glitter, aren't without their cracks, and they certainly aren't immortal. So, armed with a pen, ChatGPT, a pot of coffee, and an overworked armchair, I embarked on a quest to envisage what could keep these systems ticking over, not just for a few election cycles, but for a good five centuries. A tall order, you might say, and you'd be right.

The chosen champions in this epic were none other than representative democracy and market capitalism. They're dissected, analyzed, and finally praised in books three and six of this series. But let's not get ahead of ourselves and label them as 'ideal' just yet. They need a sturdy foundation, and this proved to be a simpler choice. I began with the enlightenment virtues and constitutional liberalism, laying the first bricks in books 1 and 2 for representative democracy. Then came science and reason, coupled with the joys of productive work in books 4 and 5, underpinning market capitalism.

So, there you have it – a sextet of pillars in a logical sequence: Enlightenment Virtues, Constitutional Liberalism, Representative Democracy, Science and Reason, Productive Work, and Market Capitalism. But let's not get too caught up in order. These were not written in sequence, nor need they be read as such. In fact, each of the 424 essays can stand alone and provide the basis for workshops, a testament to the interconnected yet independent nature of these themes.

Now, I hear some of you asking, "What about God, money, and family? Aren't they crucial pillars too?" Yes, indeed, stable money, a benevolent deity, and the warmth of family love are vital. But here's the thing – they are often the happy by-products of solid political systems and robust economic frameworks. So, in a way, they are already there, subtly woven into the other pillars I've chosen.

These volumes are not the be-all and end-all on these subjects. Far from it. They are more like kindling, meant to ignite discussions and debates that will hopefully blaze for centuries. My grand plan, you ask? To establish a foundation dedicated to keeping the conversation going, one essay at a time, year after year, for the next five hundred years.

In short, these six pillars are my humble offering to the ongoing dialogue of humanity, a conversation that has spanned millennia and one that I hope will continue long after my final curtain call.

ANTONIO J. MARQUES-MENDES

Index

absolute

    majority, 190
    power, 187, 233, 286
absolutism, 25, 26

administrators, 24

affluence, 25

anarchy, 25, 26, 158, 302

arbitrators, 24

Athens, 22, 37, 144

authoritarian, 15, 16, 25,
    34, 36, 42, 91, 102,
    136, 137, 218, 225,
    227, 233, 235

Big Brother, 22

Britain, 36, 39, 40, 76

British, 17, 41, 168

capitalism, 18, 21, 25,
27, 33, 34, 35, 36, 42,
44, 90, 91, 135, 148,
198, 201, 206, 208,
225, 231, 233, 234,
235, 236, 237, 249,
264, 265, 272, 273,
274, 286, 288, 291,
300, 307, 309, 310,
311

central planning

    communism, 25, 27
ChatGPT, vii, 17

checks and balances, 40,
    52, 62, 63, 64, 95,
    101, 253, 257

Chinese, 34, 211, 218

civilization, 25, 85, 92,
    93, 117

climate change, 22, 153,
    318

References

Applebaum, Anne (2020), Twilight of Democracy: The Failure of Politics and the Parting of Friends. Kindle Edition

Bastiat, Frédéric (1850), La Loi (The Law),

Bernstein, Edouard (1899), Die Voraussetzungen des Sozialismus (),

Brooker, Charlie (2011-2023), television series: Black Mirror,

Dick, Philip K. (1956), The Minority Report,

Freeland, Chrystia (2012), Plutocrats: The Rise of the New Global Super-Rich and the Fall of Everyone Else,

Hayek, (1944), Road to Serfdom,

Hamilton, Alexander, Jay, John, and Madison, James (1787-1788) the Federalist Papers, is a series of 85 essays written between October 1787 and May 1788.

Heinlein, Robert A. (1987), Starship Troopers,

Jencks, Christopher (2004), Our Unequal Democracy, https://prospect.org/special-report/unequal-democracy/

Judt, Tony (2006), Postwar: A History of Europe Since 1945,

Kant, Emmanuel (1795), Perpetual Peace: A Philosophical Sketch,

Keynes, J.M. (1936), General Theory,

Layard, R. (2005). Happiness: lessons form a New Science. London: Allen Lane. Penguin UK.

Luxembourg, Rosa (1899), Social Reform or Revolution? (German: Sozialreform oder Revolution?)

Maddison, A. (2005). Growth and interaction in the world economy. The Roots of Modernity, Washington DC.

Marques-Mendes, A.J. (2011), Short Essays in Economics and Finance, CreateSpace.

Marques-Mendes, A.J. (2016), The Beauty of Capitalism: And why it thrives despite its many critics (The six pillars for the good of humanity Book 1) Kindle Edition, CreateSpace.

Masterson, Matt (2023), 'ComEd Four' Found Guilty of Conspiring to Bribe Former Illinois House Speaker Michael Madigan, May 2, 2023 6:08 pm https://news.wttw.com/2023/05/02/jurors-reach-verdict-comed-four-bribery-case

More, Thomas (1516), 'Utopia',

OECD (2010), Principles for Transparency and Integrity in Lobbying,

https://legalinstruments.oecd.org/public/doc/256/25
6.en.pdf.

Rand, A. (1964). The virtue of selfishness. Penguin.

Rånge, M. & Sandberg, M. (2014). "Civilizations" and Political-Institutional Paths: A Sequence Analysis of the MaxRange2 Data Set, 1789 – 2013. In: : . Paper presented at 110th APSA (American Political Science Association) Annual Meeting 2014, Washington D.C., USA, August 28–31, 2014 (pp. 1-46).

Schumpeter, Joseph (1942), Capitalism, Socialism, and Democracy,

Shea, Robert, Wilson, Robert A. (1975), The Illuminatus! Trilogy,

Smith, L. Neil (1979), The Probability Broach,

Wells, H.G. (1895), The Time Machine,

Wolf, Martin (2010), what-is-the-role-of-the-state, FT, http://blogs.ft.com/martin-wolf-exchange/2010/08/08/what-is-the-role-of-the-state/